Claude M.
Bristol

THE
MAGIC OF
BELIEVING

The science of setting your goal
and then reaching it

A FIRESIDE BOOK
Published by Simon & Schuster
New York London Toronto Sydney Tokyo Singapore

"If thou can'st believe, all things are possible to him that believeth."

Mark 9:23

FIRESIDE
Simon & Schuster Building
Rockefeller Center
1230 Avenue of the Americas
New York, New York 10020

Library of Congress Cataloging-in-Publication Data

Bristol, Claude M. (Claude Myron), 1891–1951.
The magic of believing.

Includes index.
1. Telepathy. 2. Success. I. Title.
BF1171.B865 1985   131   84-24990

ISBN 0-671-76411-X

Contents

Foreword

You're about to read a classic book read by millions and regarded as an all-time bestseller.

In 1966, I first came to the United States of America to attend college. I had set foot in the land of opportunity, but I was alone and without money and spoke very few words of English. I felt the odds were against me. How would I live? How would I pay for school? I began to feel discouraged.

Yet I remembered something my mother used to say to me when I was a little boy: "If you want to be great, you must walk with people who are great." She meant that if you want to be happy, hang around people who are happy. If you want to be successful, hang around successful people. If you want to awaken the genius inside you, then hang around people who are in touch with great ideas. And study books of greatness.

So I took my mother's advice. To learn the systems of success, I sought out successful people who gave me keys for getting what I wanted out of life. Time and again, high achievers would recommend that I read *The Magic of Believing*. I picked up a copy and found myself on a journey of exploration and personal growth.

Claude Bristol's book gave me the encouragement and support that I needed. It shows in a very simple but persuasive way how the law of suggestion can be used to improve effectiveness in everything we do. It unlocked my potential to believe in myself and gave me a whole arsenal of effective techniques for developing and sustaining that belief. For instance, Bristol tells how he used to doodle dollar signs on every piece of paper that came across his desk. Sound strange? Well, far from being a mindless exercise, it's a deliberate technique of visualization aimed squarely at enforcing the power of belief. Take it from me, it works!

Literally thousands of companies and individuals have used Bristol's "card device" to reach their goals. I also use Bristol's "mirror technique" and frequently recommend it in my speeches and seminars. But this book is not simply a collection of motivational tricks. The techniques are important because they serve and support the magic of believing.

In every arena of life, there are winners and losers. What makes the difference can be summarized in one word: *belief!* Bristol knows that people can become what they contemplate. He shows how what he refers to as "mental picture-making" can transform subconscious thoughts into practical actions. He argues you to take the initiative in life—an instinctively positive attitude characteristic of people who believe in themselves and who succeed. Most of history's greatest achievements have been accomplished not by the most talented but by the people who were willing to take on great risks and challenges and see them through. And that happens only by believing.

Get ready to explore, as I have, the potential of your mind power. Prepare to learn from Claude Bristol about the incredible magic of believing. All of us can develop belief, but few of us know how. You can become the unique person that it is in you to become, but only if you resist the urge to conform to the images others hold for you. Only if you are willing to dream . . . and believe. The more you believe in yourself, the greater will be your achievements. And that's what *The Magic of Believing* is all about. Don't read it only because you want to understand others. Read it because you want to apply the magic of believing in your personal and professional life.

No, Claude Bristol's book is not an ordinary work. It's extraordinary. It contains the proven secret for setting your goals and reaching them. As Bristol suggests: Read and reread the book until it becomes a part of your daily life. Then, when you know you can tackle the challenges of life, you can turn all your potential into reality.

NIDO R. QUBEIN

A nationally known speaker, author, and consultant to some of North America's corporate giants, Nido R. Qubein is past president of the National Speakers Association and the recipient of many prestigious awards. He lives in High Point, North Carolina.

This book is affectionately dedicated . . .

to Dr. R. C. W.
who gave me the first clue

to L. B. N.
who persuaded me to use it

to E. L. B.
who is a part of it

to V. P. C. and W. C. B.
*without whose urgings this book would
never have been written*

to Merton S. Yewdale
whose friendly advice and enthusiasm were a constant inspiration

and to
the memories of great independent thinkers of all times.

chapter one

How I came to tap the power of belief

Is there some force, or factor, or power, or science—call it what you will—which a few people understand and use to overcome their difficulties and achieve outstanding success? I firmly believe that there is, and it is my purpose in this book to try to explain it so that you can use it if you desire.

Around 1933 the financial editor of a great Los Angeles newspaper attended lectures I gave to financial men in that city and read my brochure *T.N.T.—It Rocks the Earth*. Afterwards, he wrote,

"You have caught from the ether something that has a mystical quality—a something that explains the magic of coincidence, the mystery of what makes men lucky."

I realized that I had run across something that was practical and workable. But I didn't consider it then (neither do I now) as anything mystical, except in the sense that it is unknown to the majority of people. This "something" has always been known to a fortunate few down the centuries, but for some unknown reason it is still barely understood by the average person.

Years ago, when I started to teach this science by means of lectures and my brochure, I wasn't certain that the concepts could be grasped by the ordinary individual. But since then, I have seen those who have used it to double and triple their incomes, build their own successful businesses, acquire homes of their dreams, and create sizable fortunes. I am now convinced that any intelligent person who is sincere with himself can reach any heights he desires. I had no intention of writing a second book, although many urged me to do so. But a few months ago, a woman in the book business who had sold many copies of my first little book literally read me the riot act:

"You have a duty to give to the men and women who seek places for themselves in the world, in easily understood form, the new material that you have given in your lectures. Everyone of ambition wants to get ahead, and you have amply demonstrated that you have something that will help anyone. It's up to you to pass it along."

It took time to sell myself on the idea. But having served as a soldier in World War I, mostly in France and Germany, and having been active for many years in ex-service men's organizations as well as a state commission for the rehabilitation of ex-service men and women, I realized that it would be hard for many individuals to make outstanding places for themselves in a world from which they had long been separated. It is with a sincere desire to help them, as well as all ambitious men and women, that I write this more full and detailed exposition of the Power of Belief. Thus this work is written also to help develop individual thinking and doing.

Since this book may fall into the hands of some who may call me a crackpot or screwball, let me say that I am past the half-century mark and have had many years of hard practical business experience—as well as a goodly number of years as a newspaper man. I started as a police reporter. Police reporters are trained to get facts and take nothing for granted. For a two-year period I was church editor of a large metropolitan newspaper, during which I came in close contact with clergymen and leaders of all sects and denominations, mind-healers, divine healers, Spiritualists, Christian Scientists, New Thought-ers, Unity leaders, sun and idol worshipers—and, yes, even a few infidels and pagans.

The well-known English evangelist Gypsy Smith was making a tour of America at that time. Night after night as I sat on his platform, watching people stumble down the aisles, some sobbing, others shouting hysterically, I wondered. . . .

Again I wondered when I accompanied the police in answering a riot call: some Holy Rollers in a moment of hysteria had knocked over a stove and set fire to their meeting hall. When I attended my first (and only) meeting of Shakers, I wondered—as I did while attending various spiritualistic meetings. I wondered as I heard the testimonials at the Christian Scientists' Wednesday night meetings. I wondered when I watched a group of people immersed in the icy waters of a mountain stream and coming up shouting "Hallelujah!" even though their teeth were chattering. I wondered at the Indians' ceremonial dances and their rain-dance rituals. Billy Sunday also caused me to wonder as, in later years, did Aimee Semple McPherson.

In France during the First World War, I marveled at the simple faith of the peasants and the powers of their village *curées*. I heard stories of miracles at Lourdes, and of somewhat similar miracles at other shrines. When in a famous old Roman church, I saw elderly men and women climb literally on their knees up a long flight of stairs to gaze upon a holy urn—a climb that is no simple task for an athletically trained young person—I wondered again.

Business brought me into contact with the Mormons, and when I heard the story of Joseph Smith and the revelations on the plates of gold, I was again given to wonder. The Dukhobors of western Canada, who would doff their clothes when provoked, likewise made me wonder. While in Hawaii I heard much about the powers of the kahunas who could, it was claimed, cause people to die or live by praying. The great powers attributed to these kahunas profoundly impressed me.

In my early days as a newspaper man, I saw a famous medium try to make "spirits" respond before a crowded courtroom of antagonistic scoffers. The judge had promised to release the medium if he could get the "spirits" to speak in the courtroom. Yet they failed to materialize, and I wondered why—because the medium's followers had testified to remarkable séances.

Many years later, I was commissioned to write a series of articles on what the police call the "fortune-telling racket." I visited everyone from gypsy phrenologists to crystal-ball gazers, from astrologers to spiritualistic mediums. I heard what purported to be the voices of old Indian "guides" tell me the past, the present, and the future, and I heard from relatives I never knew existed.

Several times I have been in a hospital room in which people around me died, while others with seemingly worse ailments were up and—apparently—fully recovered within a short time. I have known of partially paralyzed people who got over their condition in a matter of days. I have known people who claim to have cured their rheumatism or arthritis by wearing a copper band around their wrists—others by mental healing. From relatives and close friends I have heard stories of how warts on hands suddenly disappeared. I am familiar with the stories of those who permit rattlesnakes to bite them and still live; and with hundreds of other tales of mysterious happenings and healings.

Moreover, I have made myself familiar with the lives of great men and women of history and have met and interviewed many outstanding men and women in all lines of human endeavor. Often I have wondered just what it was that took them to the top. I have seen coaches take seemingly inferior baseball and football teams and infuse them with something that caused them to win. In the Depression days, I saw badly whipped sales organizations do an abrupt about-face and bring in more business than ever before.

Apparently I was born with a huge bump of curiosity, for I have always had an insatiable yearning to seek answers and explanations. This quest has taken me to many strange places, brought to light many peculiar cases, and caused me to read every book I could get my hands on dealing with religions, cults, and physical and mental sciences. I have read literally thousands of books on modern psychology, metaphysics, ancient magic, Voodoo, Yoga, Theosophy, Christian Science, Unity, Truth, New Thought, Couéism, and many others dealing with what I call "Mind Stuff," as well as the philosophies and teachings of great masters of the past.

Many were nonsensical, others strange, and many very profound. Gradually I discovered that a golden thread runs through all the teachings and makes them work for those who sincerely accept and apply them, and that thread can be named in the single word *belief.* It is this same element or factor—belief—that causes people to be cured through mental healing, enables others to climb high the ladder of success, and gets phenomenal results for all who accept it. *Why* belief works miracles is something that cannot be satisfactorily explained; but have no doubt that there's genuine magic in believing. "The magic of believing" became a phrase around which my thoughts steadily revolved.

I am convinced that the so-called secret fraternal organizations guard a real "royal secret" which very few members ever grasp. The conclusion must be that "no mind ever receives the truth until it is prepared to receive it." One order provides candidates with a very profound book (to be studied in connection with the degree work), which itself would be practically an open-sesame to life if the candidates could understand and follow its tenets. But few read it, complaining that "it is too deep" for them. I am convinced, too, that some of these organizations, like many secret orders which possess a knowledge and understanding of life, use parables and misinterpretations to mislead.

When *T.N.T.—It Rocks the Earth* was first published, I imagined that it would be easily understood since I had written it simply. But as the years went by, some readers protested that it was too much in digest form. Others said they couldn't understand it. I had assumed that most people knew something about the power of thought. Now I realize that I was mistaken, and those who had an understanding of the subject were comparatively few. Later, over many years of lecturing before clubs, business and sales organizations, I discovered that most people were vitally interested in the subject, but that it had to be fully explained. Finally, I undertook to write this book in words that anyone can understand—and with the hope that it will help many to reach their goals in life.

The science of thought it as old as man himself. The wise men of all ages have known it and used it. The only thing I have done is to put the subject in modern language and bring to the reader's attention what some of today's outstanding minds are doing to substantiate the great truths that have come down through the centuries.

Fortunately for the world, people are coming to the realization that there is something to this "mind-stuff" after all. I believe that millions of people would like to get a better understanding of it—and prove that it *does* work.

Therefore, let me start by relating a few experiences from my own life, with the hope that they will give you a better understanding of the entire science.

Early in 1918, I landed in France as a "casual" soldier, unattached to a regular company. As a result, it was several weeks before my service record (necessary for my pay) caught up with me. During that period I had no money to buy gum, candy, cigarettes, and the like, since the few dollars I had before sailing had been spent at the transport ship's canteen to relieve the monotony of the regular menu. Every time I saw a man light a cigarette or chew a stick of gum, it reminded me that I was without money to spend on myself. Certainly, I was eating, and the army clothed me and provided me with a place on the ground to sleep, but I grew bitter at having no spending money and no way of getting any. One night en-route to the forward area on a crowded troop train when sleep was out of the question, I made up my mind that on my return to civilian life, I would have a *lot* of money. The whole pattern of my life was altered at that moment.

True, I had been something of a reader in my youth; the Bible had been a must in our family. As a boy I was interested in wireless telegraphy, X-rays, high-frequency apparatus, and similar manifestations of electricity, and I had read every book on these subjects I could find. But while I was familiar with such terms as radiation frequencies, vibrations, oscillations, magnetic influences, etc., in those days they meant nothing to me outside of the strictly electrical field. Perhaps my first inkling of a connection between the mind and electrical or vibratory influences came when upon my completing law school, an instructor gave me an old book, Thomson Jay Hudson's *Law of Psychic Phenomena* I read it, but only superficially. Either I did not understand it, or my mind was not ready to receive its profound truths. On that fateful night in the spring of 1918, when I told myself that some day I would have a lot of money, I did not realize that I was laying the groundwork for a series of causes which would unleash forces that would bring accomplishment. As a matter of fact, the idea never entered my mind that I could develop a fortune with my thinking and believing.

My Army classification card listed me as a newspaper man. I had been attending an Army Training School to qualify for a commission, but the whole training-school program was discontinued just as we finished the course; thus most of us landed in France as enlisted men. However, I considered myself a qualified journalist and felt that there was a better place for me in the American Expeditionary Force. Yet like many others, I found myself pushing wheelbarrows and lugging heavy shells and other ammunition.

Then one night at an ammunition depot near Toul, things began to happen. I was ordered to appear before the Commanding Officer, who asked me whom I knew at First Army Headquarters. I didn't know a soul there and didn't even know where it was located, and I told him so. Then he showed me orders directing me to report there immediately. A car and driver were provided, and the next morning found me at First Army Headquarters in charge of a daily progress bulletin. I was answerable only to a colonel.

During the months that followed, I frequently thought about the commission to which I was entitled. Then the links began to form into a chain. One day, entirely out of a clear sky, came orders transferring me to the *Stars and Stripes*, the Army newspaper; I had long had an ambition to be on its staff, but had done nothing about it. The next day, as I was preparing to leave for Paris, I was called before the colonel who showed me a telegram signed by the Adjutant General's office at GHQ, asking if I was available for commission. The colonel asked whether I would rather have a commission than report to the Army newspaper. Foreseeing that the war would soon end and I would be happier among other newspaper men, I said I would prefer the transfer to the *Stars and Stripes*. I never learned who was responsible for the telegram, but obviously something was working in my behalf.

Following the armistice, my desire to get out of the Army became insistent. I wanted to begin building that fortune. But the *Stars and Stripes* did not suspend publication until the summer of 1919, and it was August before I got home. However, the forces I had unconsciously set in motion were already setting the stage for me.

About nine-thirty the next morning after my arrival home, I received a telephone call from the president of a club in which I had been active. He told me to call a prominent man in the investment banking business who had read about my return and had expressed a wish to see me before I resumed newspaper work. I called the man and, two days later, embarked upon a long career as an investment banker, which later led me to the vice-presidency of a well-known Pacific Coast firm.

While my salary was smart at the start, I realized that I was in a business where there were many opportunities to make money. Just how I was to make it was then not revealed, but I just knew that I would have that fortune I had in mind. In less than ten years, I did have it, and not only was it sizable, but I was a substantial stockholder in the company and had several outside profitable interests. During those years I had constantly before me a mental picture of wealth.

Many people in moments of abstraction or while talking on the telephone engage in doodling—drawing or sketching odd designs and patterns upon paper. My doodling was in the form of dollar signs like these—$$$$$—$$$—$$—$$$$—on every paper that came across my desk. The cardboard covers of all the files placed before me daily were scrawled with these markings, as were the covers of telephone directories, scratch-pads, and even the face of important correspondence. I want my readers to remember this detail, because it suggests the mechanics to be used in applying this magic which I'll explain in detail later.

During the past years, I have found that by far the greatest problems bothering most people are financial ones.

With today's intense competition, millions are facing the same kinds of problems. However, it matters little to what ends this science is used. It will be effective in achieving the object of your desire—and in this connection, let me tell another experience.

Shortly after the idea of *T.N.T.—It Rocks the Earth* came to me but before I put it on paper, I took a trip to the Orient and sailed on the *Empress of Japan*, noted for its excellent cuisine. In my travels through Canada and in Europe I had developed a fondness for Trappist cheese made by the Trappist monks of Quebec. When I couldn't find it on the ship's menu, I laughingly complained to the chief steward that I had sailed on his ship only to get some of the famous "Trappist" cheese. He replied that he was sorry, but there was none aboard.

The more I thought about it, the more I hungered for some of that cheese. One night a ship's party was held. Upon returning to my cabin quarters after midnight, I found a big table had been set up in one of the rooms. On it was the largest cheese I had ever seen. It was "Trappist" cheese.

Later I asked the chief steward where he found it. "I was certain we had none aboard when you first mentioned it," he answered, "but you seemed so set on having some, I made up my mind to search through all the ship's stores. We found it in the emergency storeroom in the bottom of the hold." Something was working for me on that trip, too, for I had no claim to anything but ordinary service. However, I sat at the executive officer's table and was frequently his personal guest in his quarters, as well as on inspection trips through the ship.

Naturally the treatment I received made a great impression on me, and in Honolulu, I often thought how nice it would be to receive comparable attention on my journey home on another ship. One afternoon I got the sudden impulse to leave for the mainland. It was about closing time when I appeared at the ticket agency to ask what reservations I could get. A ship was leaving the next day at noon, and I purchased the only remaining cabin ticket.

The next day, just a few minutes before noon, as I started up the gangplank, I said to myself in an offhand manner, "They treated you as a king on the *Empress of Japan*. The least you can do here is to sit at the captain's table. Sure, you'll sit at the captain's table."

The ship got under way. As we steamed out of the harbor, the dining-room steward asked passengers to appear in the dining room for assignment to tables. When I came before him, about half the assignments had been made. He asked for my ticket, glanced at it and then at me, saying, "Oh yes, table A, seat No. 5." It was the captain's table, and I was seated directly across from him. Aboard that ship, many things happened which pertain to the subject of this book, the most prominent being a party supposed to be in honor of my birthday—just an idea of the captain's, because my birthday was actually months away.

Later, when I found myself lecturing, I thought it would be wise to get a letter from the captain substantiating the story and I wrote him. He replied, "Sometimes as we go through life, instinctively we get the idea to do this or that. That noon I was sitting in the doorway of my cabin watching the passengers come up the gangplank, and as you came aboard, something told me to seat you at my table. Beyond that I cannot explain, any more than I can explain how I can frequently stop my ship at the right spot at the pier at the first try."

People who have heard the story—and who know nothing about the magic of believing—have declared that it was mere coincidence that the captain selected me. I am positive it wasn't, and I'm also certain that this captain (who knows quite a bit about this science) will agree with me. Aboard that ship were dozens of people far more important than I could ever be. I carried nothing to set me apart, being one of those who can pass in a crowd. So obviously it wasn't the clothes I wore or the way I looked that prompted the captain to pick me out of several hundred passengers to receive personal attention.

In presenting to you this very workable science, I am aware that the subject has been handled before from many angles, but also realize that many people shy away from any approach that smacks of religion, the occult, or the metaphysical. Accordingly, I am using the language of a business-man who believes that sincere thinking, clear writing, and simple language will get any message across.

You have often heard it said that you can if you believe you can. An old Latin proverb says, "Believe that you have it, and you have it." Belief is the motivating force that enables you to achieve your goal. If you are ill and imbedded deeply within you is the thought or belief that you will recover, the odds are that you will. It's the belief or the basic confidence within you that brings outward material results. I speak of normal and mentally healthy people. I wouldn't tell a handicapped person that he could excel in baseball or football. Nor would I tell a woman who was quite plain-looking that she could make herself into a great beauty overnight, since the odds are against it. Yet these things *could* happen, for there have been many remarkable cures. And when more is learned about the powers of the mind, I firmly believe that we shall witness many cures that today's medical profession deems impossible. Finally, I would never discourage anyone; for in this life, anything can happen—and what can help bring it to pass is Hope.

Dr. Alexander Cannon was a distinguished British scientist and physician whose books on the general subject of thought stirred up controversy here and abroad. He declared that while today a man cannot grow a new leg (as a crab can grow a new claw), he could if the mind of man hadn't rejected the possibility. The eminent scientist claimed that if the thought is changed in the innermost depths of the unconscious mind, then man will grow a new leg as easily as the crab grows a new claw. I know, such a statement may sound incredible, but how do we know that it will not be done some day?

Frequently I lunch with a group of medical men, all specialists in various branches of medicine and surgery. I know that if I voiced such an idea, they would suggest that I have my head examined. However, I find that some of these doctors, especially those more recently graduated from our better schools, are no longer closing their minds to the role that thought plays in causing and curing functional disturbances in the body.

A few weeks before I wrote this chapter, a neighbor came to me to explain how his warts happened to disappear. During a stay at the hospital, he had wandered out on the porch where another convalescent patient was conversing with a friend. Said the visitor to the other patient, "So you would like to get rid of the warts on your hand? Well, just let me count them, and they'll disappear."

My neighbor said he looked at the stranger for a moment, then said: "While you're about it, will you count mine, too?" He did, and my neighbor thought no more about it until after he had gone home and he happened to look at his hands one day. "The mess of warts had entirely disappeared!" he told me.

I told this story to a group of doctors one day. A well-known specialist—and personal friend—grunted, saying, "Preposterous!" Across the table, another doctor who had recently been teaching in a medical school came to my aid, declaring that there were many authenticated cases of suggestion having been used to cure warts.

I was tempted to remind them that several years before, newspapers and medical journals had reported how Heim, a Swiss geologist, had removed warts by suggestion, and had also cited the procedure of Professor Block, another Swiss specialist, in his use of psychology and suggestion for the same purpose. Back in January, 1945, Columbia University's College of Physicians and Surgeons set up the first psychoanalytic and psychosomatic clinic in this country for the purpose of studying the relationship between the unconscious mind and the body. I kept silent, feeling that I was too outnumbered for an argument.

Since this conversation, considerable publicity was given to the findings of Dr. Frederick Kalz, a noted Canadian authority who flatly stated that suggestion works in many cases, even to curing warts that are infectious and caused by a virus. In a 1945 article in the *Canadian Medical Association Journal*, Dr. Kalz declared that, "In every country in the world some magic procedures to cure warts are known . . . It may be anything from covering the wart with spider-webs to burying toad eggs on a crossroad at new moon; all these magic procedures are effective, if the patient *believes in them*." In describing the treatment of patients with skin trouble, he says, "I have often prescribed the very same ointment, accompanied by some promising words, which has been tried unsuccessfully by some other medical man, and got credit for a quick cure." He also points out that X-ray therapy is especially suggestive; it works even when the technician fails to switch on the high power! Experiments with systematic fake irradiation bear out this observation. Here in Dr. Kalz's work we see actual examples of the *magic of believing* at work in the curing of warts and the treatment of skin trouble.

Another time my medical friends and I were discussing telepathy. I remarked that some of our greatest students and scholars believed in it. Dr. Alexis Carrel, of the Rockefeller Institute for Medical Research, was not only a thorough believer in the phenomenon but declared that there was definite scientific proof that man could project his thought even at great distances into other minds.

"Oh, he was just a senile old man," remarked another specialist at the table, a nationally known member of the American Medical Association.

I looked at him with astonishment, for Dr. Carrel won the Nobel Prize for his medical research. When he put forth his ideas in that remarkable book, *Man the Unknown*, published in 1935, he was regarded as one of the world's foremost medical scientists and investigators.

I have no quarrel with the medical fraternity. Quite the contrary, for its members are generally sincere, able, and open-minded men, and a number are among my closest friends. However, some medical specialists, especially those inclined to restrict their studies to their respective fields, refuse to accept anything that may upset their early teachings and dogmatic beliefs. This resistance is not confined to the medical profession: countless specialists in other lines, including business, know very little outside of their chosen fields, and their minds are closed to any idea beyond their limited imaginations. Frequently, I have offered to lend books to these various specialists—only to be told, after informing them of the contents, that they were not interested.

Paradoxically, many apparently well-educated men and women, successful in their respective fields, will, in their broad ignorance, condemn the idea of thought power and make no endeavor to learn more about it—*yet every one of them has unconsciously made use of it!* Again, many people will believe only what they like to believe or what fits into their own scheme of things, summarily rejecting anything to the contrary. Countless men whose ideas developed the very civilization we live in have been hooted at, slandered, even crucified by the ignoramuses of their times. I think of the words of Marie Corelli, the English novelist who became world famous in the 19th century:

> *The very idea that any one creature (human) should be fortunate enough to secure some particular advantage which others, through their own indolence or indifference, have missed is sufficient to excite the envy of the weak or the anger of the ignorant . . . It is impossible that an outsider should enter into a clear understanding of the mystical spiritual-nature world around him, and it follows that the teachings and tenets of that spiritual-nature world must be more or less a closed book to such a one—a book, moreover, which he seldom cares or dares to try and open. For this reason, the sages concealed much of their profound knowledge from the multitude, because they rightly recognized the limitations of narrow minds and prejudiced opinions . . . What the fool cannot learn, he laughs at, thinking that by his laughter he shows superiority instead of latent idiocy.**

---

*From *The Life Everlasting* by Marie Corelli, Borden Publishing Co., Los Angeles.

Great investigators and thinkers of the world, including many famous scientists, are in the open today, freely discussing the subject and giving the results of their experiments. Shortly before his death, Charles P. Steinmetz, famous engineer of the General Electric Company, declared, "The most important advance in the next fifty years will be in the realm of the spiritual—dealing with the spirit—thought." Dr. Robert Gault, while professor of Psychology at Northwestern University, was credited with the statement: "We are at the threshold of our knowledge of the latent psychic powers of man."

Much has been written and said about mystical powers, unknown forces, the occult, metaphysics (beyond science), mental physics, psychology (the science of mind), black and white magic, and many kindred subjects, causing most people to believe that they are in the field of the supernatural. Perhaps they are for some. But to me, the only inexplicable thing about these powers is that belief makes them work.

During the years that I have appeared before luncheon clubs, business concerns, and sales organizations, as well as talking over the radio to thousands of people about this science, I have seen results that can be termed phenomenal.

As I said before, many have used it in their business to double, treble, even quadruple their incomes. My files are filled with letters from people in all walks of life, testifying what they have accomplished by using the science. As an instance, I think of Ashley C. Dixon, whose name was once known to thousands of radio listeners in the Pacific Northwest. A number of years ago, he wrote me voluntarily to say that he had studied this subject in an academic way, but had never fully believed it until he was forty-three, when he had only $65 to his name, no employment, and no jobs available. He set out to prove to himself that the science would work. I quote the following excerpts from Mr. Dixon's letter:

"Your book *T.N.T.* put forth in workable form all that I had known before. It was like seeing Niagara Falls for the first time. One knew there was such a place; but confirmation was the actual personal contact with it. And so, *T.N.T.* gave me in print the facts I had known and used, but in a clear form. Here was something I could read and use day by day, holding the thoughts till they were fully demonstrated.

"What has all this been worth to me in dollars and cents? That, of course, is the question of the average man. He wants to see something . . . in the profit column; something material in the way of dollars and cents. Here's the answer. I have made a hundred thousand dollars, most of it in paid-up insurance and annuities. I have sold my business which costs me $5,000 (originally borrowed) for $30,000, and am now working on a contract to run for the next ten years which will net me $50,000 if I loaf; and more if I care to work. This is not a boast. It is a factual statement of what has actually happened in the past ten years . . . It cannot be done in a moment, or a day or a month, but it *can* be done."

In 1934, during the lowest point of the Depression, the head of the Better Business Bureau in a large Pacific Coast city heard of what was happening to firms and individuals who were following my teachings. He decided to investigate my work. Later he congratulated me publicly and subsequently wrote me as follows:

"My statement—that the teachings have done more to stimulate business here during the past year than any other single factor or agency—is based upon statements by numerous executives who have been using the theme successfully in their businesses . . . When I first heard of the phenomenal results you were obtaining, I was inclined to question the facts. They seemed too preposterous to be true. But upon investigation, talking with heads of firms using the theme and with salesmen who have doubled and trebled their incomes, as well as hearing many of your lectures and getting into the subject for myself, the terrific and dynamic force embraced by it all becomes apparent. It isn't going to be understood by everyone in a minute, but firms and individuals that accept what you have to give and follow through can expect some startling and extraordinary results. You have fully demonstrated that, and therefore are to be congratulated."

This man has since risen to great heights in the business world and has written me of having seen other practical demonstrations of the workings of this science.

When I started this book, I decided to check with some of the individuals and firms who had written me to certify the phenomenal results they had achieved by using this science. Without exception, every one testified to the continuing progress he had made. One of the most outstanding accounts was related by Mr. Dorr Quayle, once well-known to the Disabled American War Veterans, who was long active in veterans' affairs in the Northwest. In 1937, he wrote me:

"It was no easy matter, at first, to completely accept your ideas. But my circumstances and physical condition forced me to keep at it continuously until understanding came. . . . You see, in February, 1924, I was stricken with partial paralysis of my lower limbs. I needed crutches to even get about at all, and at best, for only short distances, and at a snail's pace. For [a bank executive] who had been active in the business world this forced inactivity was not easy to get used to. It was bearable only because I received government compensation—my disability being considered due to service during the World War. However, in 1933, the Government dropped me from the compensation rolls, and I was forced to make a living. My home and other properties were about to be repossessed. It was not a pleasant picture, nor a hopeful future.

"Necessity forced me to put into practice the principles you explained so well. Sticking to it proves them. Possibly I was favored because I couldn't quit the insurance and public accounting business—due to my inability to enter any other kind of work. But persistence gives confidence, and continued right mental attitude followed by consistent action will bring success. I haven't reached the degree of success I desire, but that does not bother me at all, for now I am making a good living, have saved my properties, and know the formula that leads to the fullest success. When you have that knowing *inside* you, fear vanishes, as do the obstructions to a continued life of all good."

I first met Mr. Quayle just after he had started his business with one desk in the front of a plumbing shop. In the following years, it was a pleasure to see him move from place to place, his business growing by leaps and bounds, until he occupied the entire ground floor of a building on one of the main thoroughfares of a great western city. Realizing that his story of achievement was a remarkable one, I asked permission to quote his earlier letter.

"By all means, do so," he replied, "if you think it will help others. You might add that I now have the whole quarters at 20th and Sandy and I employ twenty-two people. I have just brought the business lot between 28th and 29th on Sandy where I shall build my own office building. I sincerely wish that all people would accept your teachings."

At the time I grasped this science, I had no idea that I was later to put it into book form. My primary thought was to use it to save my own organization from bankruptcy. I was then vice-president of an investment banking firm, and we had been caught in the economic crisis and were headed for disaster.

I don't know whether I was inspired, but I dictated the first draft of my brochure in its entirety in less than five hours, without notes or references of any kind before me. At the same time the idea for the brochure came to me, the words, "cosmic consciousness," floated before my mind. They meant nothing then.

But after *T.N.T.—It Rocks the Earth* was published, it reached a woman author living in New York, who wrote me as follows:

"Seriously, I've been eating and sleeping [your] philosophy for the last ten years. It brought me to New York on no carfare; it sold my stuff to publishers when I had a lousy little job earning $30 a week . . . It took me to Europe a couple of times, and bought me silver foxes."

In the same letter, she urged me to read Dr. Richard Maurice Bucke's *Cosmic Consciousness*, declaring that it contained brilliant accounts of the actual experience of illumination. When I did, I was astounded to discover that my experience actually paralleled the illuminations listed and explained by Dr. Bucke. In the original draft of my brochure, I had described in detail my experience with "brilliant white light." But subsequently, when I showed the manuscript to a close friend, he urged me to tone down the wording: "People won't know what you are talking about in referring to that 'white light'—some may think you've gone off the deep end." Consequently, I changed it. But those of you know something about "cosmic illumination" and have read my earlier small book will catch my reference to the "light." However, the memory of that singular experience will always remain with me: in those few seconds, I received more knowledge and understanding than I had ever received in years of reading and studying.

In the same period, it came to me in a flash why my firm was going on the rocks—not because of the threatening outside happenings and events, but because of the mental attitude of our employees. We were all succumbing to mass fear-thoughts: we feared that the Depression was weakening our spirit and sweeping *everything* downhill to financial disaster. With our own thoughts of ruin, we were attracting the disaster to ourselves.

It occurred to me that to save the firm and to begin fighting the Depression itself, all I needed to do was reverse the thinking of every person connected with our organization. I set about doing that very thing. As Frank W. Camp, who wrote the introduction to my brochure declared, it was followed "by the most remarkable transformation of individuals and organization as well."

I admit that some of my statements may be ridiculed by classroom psychologists. But every day, thousands of people demonstrate for themselves that the science works. As for you, the reader, the main point to consider is whether it will work for you. The only way you can find out is to *try it yourself.*

I give you this science, in the confident knowledge that no matter how you use it, you will get results. But I do wish to repeat a warning given in my brochure: *Never use it for harmful or evil purposes.*

Since the beginning, there have been two great subtle forces in the world—good and evil. Both are terrifically powerful in their respective scopes and cycles. The basic principle operating both is *mind power*—massed mind power. Sometimes evil appears to have the upper hand, and at other times good is at the controls. It is mind power that has built empires, and we have seen how it can be used to destroy them—history has recorded the facts.

If you read this book reflectively, you will understand how the science can be used with terribly destructive force, as well as for good and constructive results. It is like many natural forces, such as water and fire, which are among men's greatest benefactors. Yet both can be hideously catastrophic, depending upon whether they are used for constructive or destructive purposes.

Therefore, take great care that you do not misuse the science of "Mind Stuff." I cannot emphasize this too strongly, for if you employ it for harmful or evil purposes, it will boomerang and destroy you just as it has others down through the centuries. These are not idle words, but solemn words of warning.

chapter two

Mind-stuff experiments

In order to get a clearer understanding of our subject, you should give some thought to thought itself and to its phenomena. No one knows what thought really is, other than some sort of mental action. But like the unknown element of electricity, we see its manifestations everywhere. We see it in the actions and expressions of a child, in an aged person, in animals, and to varying degrees in every living thing. The more we contemplate and study thought, the more we realize what a terrific force it is and how unlimited its powers are.

Glance around as you read this. If you are in a furnished room, your eyes tell you that you are looking at a number of inanimate objects. That is true so far as visual perception is concerned, but you are actually looking at thoughts or ideas which have come into materialization through the creative work of some human being. It was a thought, first, that created the furniture, fashioned the window glass, gave form to the draperies and coverings.

The automobile, the skyscraper, the great 747 jumbo jets that sweep the stratosphere, the sewing machine, the tiny pin—where did they come from originally? From that strange force—thought. As we analyze further, we realize that these achievements, and in fact all of our possessions—a thousand and one things—came as a result of creative thinking. Ralph Waldo Emerson declared that the ancestor of every action is thought; when you understand that, you begin to comprehend that our world is governed by thought, and that everything external had its counterpart originally within the mind. It is just as Buddha said many centuries ago: "All that we are is the result of what we have thought."

Your very life is your thinking—and the result of your thinking processes. Your flesh, bones, and muscles can be reduced to 70 percent water and a few chemicals of small value, but it is your mind and what you think that makes you what you are. The secret of success lies not outside, but within the thoughts of man.

Figuratively, thought makes giants out of pigmies, and often turns giants into pigmies. History is filled with accounts of how thought made weak men strong and strong men weak, and you see evidence of its working around you constantly.

You do not eat, wear clothes, run for a bus, drive your car, turn on the television, or read a newspaper—you don't even raise your arm—without a preceding thought-impulse. While you may consider the motions you make as more or less automatic, perhaps caused by some physical reflexes, behind every single step you take in life, regardless of its direction, is that formidable and powerful force—thought.

The very way you walk, the way you carry yourself, your talk, your manner of dress, all reflect your way of thinking. A slovenly carriage is an indication of slovenly thinking, whereas an alert, upright carriage is the outward sign of inward strength and confidence. What you exhibit outwardly, you are inwardly. You are the product of your own thoughts. What you believe yourself to be, you are.

Thought is the original source of all wealth, all success, all material gain, all great discoveries and inventions, and of all achievement. Without it there would be no medicine, no great museums, no great plays or novels, no modern conveniences—in fact, there would be no advance over life in the most primitive ages.

Your thoughts—those that predominate—determine your character, your career, indeed, your everyday life. Thus it becomes easy to understand what is meant by the statement that "A man's thoughts make or break him." And when you realize that there can be no action or reaction, either good or bad, without the generating force of thought initiating it, then the Biblical saying, "For whatsoever a man soweth, that shall he also reap," and Shakespeare's words, "There is nothing either good or bad, but thinking makes it so," become more intelligible.

Sir Arthur Eddington, the famous English physicist, said that to an altogether unsuspected extent, the universe in which we live is a creation of our minds; while Sir James Jeans, who was equally famous in the same field, suggested that the universe was merely a creation that resulted from the thought of some great universal mind underlying and co-ordinating all of our minds.

More recently, science has uncovered parallels between the behavior of sub-atomic particles and various tenets of Eastern metaphysics. The greatest scientists and thinkers are not only voicing the ideas of the wisest men of old, but are confirming the fundamental principle of this book.

Almost since the beginning of the human race, men have been molded by those who knew something of thought's great power. All the great religious leaders, kings, warriors, and statesmen understood this science and have known that people act as they think—and also react to the thought of others, especially when it is stronger and more convincing than their own. Accordingly, men of powerful dynamic thought have always swayed people by appealing to their minds—whether sometimes to lead them into freedom or into slavery. There never was a period in history when we had more reason to study our own thoughts, understand them, and learn how to use them to improve our lives by drawing upon the great source of power within each of us.

Undoubtedly, we become what we envisage. There was a time when I would have laughed at people who talked about the magnetic force of thought, how thought correlates with its object, how it can affect people and inanimate things even at great distances. But I no longer laugh, nor do others who know something of its power, for anyone who has any intelligence sooner or later comes to realize that thought can change the surface of the entire globe.

George Russell, the famous Irish editor and poet, was once quoted as saying that we become what we contemplate; and he certainly demonstrated it in his own life by becoming a great writer, lecturer, painter, and poet. However, it must be kept in mind that many of the thoughts we think are not ours at all, at least not of our own originating. We are molded by the thoughts of others; by what we hear in conversation, what we read in newspapers, magazines, and books, what we hear in the movies, on TV, and on the radio; even by chance remarks from bystanders. And these thoughts bombard us constantly. Some of them, which harmonize with our own inmost thoughts and open the way to greater visions in our life, are helpful. But too often these thoughts are upsetting, weaken our self-confidence, and turn us away from our higher purposes. It is these outside thoughts that are the trouble makers, and later I shall explain how you can keep free of them.

Few people give much thought to the law of cause and effect as it applies to the operation of the mind. Much less do they understand the meaning of such axioms as "Everything is within; nothing is without" or "Mind is the source of power." A superb explanation of this appeared in an article entitled "El Dorado," published in the *Commercial and Financial Chronicle* back on December 10, 1932.

El Dorado, a country rich beyond all precedent in gold and jewels, lies at every man's door. Your bonanza lies under your feet. Your luck is ready at hand. All is within; nothing is without, though it often appears that men and peoples by dumb luck or avarice or force or overreaching strike upon bonanzas and sail away in fair weather on the sea of prosperity . . . Man individually and collectively is entitled to life in all abundance. It is a most evident fact. Religion and philosophy assert it; history and science prove it. "That they might have life, and that they might have it more abundantly," is the law. What do you seek? Pay the price and take it away. There is no limit to the supply, but the more precious the thing you seek, the higher the price. For everything we obtain, we must barter the gold of our own spirits . . .

Where to find the gold of the All Powerful? One secures the gold of the spirit when he finds himself. When he finds himself, he finds freedom and all riches, achievement, and propserity. High-sounding talk? No, the most palpable evidence of American history and biography, of all history. The concrete proof is apparent even in current events if we but open our eyes. Nothing substantial, lasting, powerful, or moving was ever accomplished, nor ever can be, except by men [who have discovered] in themselves of the gold of the spirit, which commands dominion, power, and accomplishment. Men who know themselves know at once that all material things and ideas have a spiritual counterpart or basis. They see it in money, in credit. The law of supply and demand is not to an awakened man merely an economic principle, but the material manifestation of spiritual law. Such freedom-seeking men see the same principle operating in gravitation, in chemical affinities, in macrocosm and in microcosm.

America has long been the greatest of El Dorados, the stage upon which the most numerous of self-found men worked their bonanzas and their miracles of thought to the enrichment of themselves and mankind at large. There is no exploitation, only a showering of gifts, easily bought by free spirits and generously scattered on all hands according to the expressed law of bargain of the Original, Permanent Owner, and First Producer. To the self-found man of action all the money, credit, and capital goods he can use . . . Mackay, O'Brien, Hearst, and Fair, brave young Americans of 1849, found gold in themselves before they struck it rich in California. They had to. "If there is gold there," they told one another, "we'll get our share" . . . How great must have been the spiritual wealth of such a free-found man as James J. Hill, who built the Great Northern Railroad from nowhere to nowhere, in a wilderness where no one lives. His madness founded an empire. By spiritual force he turned forests and plains into a thousand El Dorados, and by the same force commanded all the gold and credit needed for the markets of Amsterdam and London and enabled millions of Americans to discover for themselves great bonanzas in the cold Northwest.

Thomas A. Edison said a few years before he died: "Ideas come from space. This may seem astonishing and impossible to believe, but it is true. Ideas come from out of space." Surely Edison should have known, for few men ever received or gave forth more ideas . . . Let each man seek the El Dorado within himself. Power is plentiful. The source is inexhaustible. As the Canonical Fathers of the church expressed it, that which is received is according to the measure of the recipient. It is not the power that is lacking, it is the will. When one finds oneself, the will becomes automatically set toward El Dorado.

By a full and powerful imagination anything can be brought into concrete form. The great physician, Paracelsus, said: "The human spirit is so great a thing that no man can express it; could we rightly comprehend the mind of man, nothing would be impossible to us upon the earth. Through faith, the imagination is invigorated and completed, for it really happens that every doubt mars its perfection. Faith must strengthen the imagination, for faith establishes the will." Faith is personal, individual. Salvation, any way you take it, is personal. Faith comes in the finding of one's self. This self-finding establishes a clear realization of one's identity with the eternal. Strong, self-assertive men built up this El Dorado of America. "Man, know theyself, thine own individual self," is everlastingly the supreme command. Self-knowers always dwell in El Dorado; they drink from the fountain of youth and are at all times owners of all they wish to enjoy.

The words of Paracelsus just quoted are well worth rereading, for once you grasp their meaning and discover how to apply the principle, you will certainly have more light on how to succeed in your undertakings. However, I must point out that hard work alone will not bring success. The world is filled with people who have worked hard but have little to show for it. Something more than hard work is necessary: namely, creative thinking and firm belief in your ability to execute your ideas. The successful people in history have succeeded through their thinking. Their hands were merely helpers to their brains.

Another important point: For success, it is essential that your desire be an all-obsessing one, your thoughts and aims be co-ordinated, and your energy be concentrated and applied without letup. It may be that you want riches or fame or position or knowledge, for each person has his own idea of what success means. But whatever you consider it to be, you can have your objective, provided you are willing to make it the burning desire of your life.

A big order, you say? Not at all. By using the dynamic force of believing, you can set all your inner forces in motion, and they in turn will help you reach your goal. If you are married, you remember the stimulating and emotional experience of courting the person you wanted for your spouse. Certainly it wasn't nerve-racking work—quite the contrary, you'll admit—but what were you using, if not this very same science, even though unconsciously? From the time you got the idea until your marriage, the desire to win a partner was uppermost in your mind. The thought, the belief, was with you every minute of the day, and perhaps in your dreams as well.

Now that you have a clearer picture of the roles that thought and desire play in your daily life, the first thing to determine is precisely what you *do* want. Starting out with the general idea that you simply want to be a success—as most people do—is too vague. You must have a pattern clearly drawn in your mind. Ask yourself, Where are you headed? What is your exact goal? Have you visualized just what you really want? If success is to be measured in terms of wealth, can you fix the amount in figures? If in terms of achievement, can you specify it definitely?

You must ask these questions, for in their answers are factors which will determine your whole life from now on. Strange as it may seem, not one out of a hundred people can answer these questions! Most people have a general desire to succeed, but beyond that, everything is indefinite. They merely go along from day to day, figuring that if they have a job today, they will have it tomorrow—and that somehow, they will be looked after in their old age. They are like corks floating aimlessly on the water, drawn this way and that by various currents, either washing up on shore or becoming water-logged and eventually sinking.

Therefore, it is vital that you know exactly what you want out of life. You must know where you are headed, and keep a fixed goal in view. That, of course, is the over-all picture; it makes no difference whether you want *a* job or a *better* one, a new house, a place in the country, or just a new pair of shoes. You must have a fixed idea before you'll obtain what you are after.

Remember, there is a great difference between a need and a desire. You may *need* a new car for driving to work, and you may *desire* one in order to give pleasure to your family. The one for business you will buy as a matter of necessity. The one for your family you will plan to get as soon as possible. For this car, you will read brochures and visit a number of dealers, because it is a model you have never had before, something that will add to your responsibilities and compel you to seek new powers of judgment within yourself and new resources outside. Desire for something new, something different, that is going to change your life, makes you exert an extra effort. And the *power of believing* alone sets in motion those inner forces by which you add what I call *plus-values* to your life.

So if you ever hope to achieve anything or gain more than you have now, begin with desire. It is the prime motivating force in all of us and, without an all-consuming desire, nothing can be achieved or gained. However, as you shall see, there is more to it than mere desire.

I am aware that metaphysicians claim that thoughts are things. They may be in a general sense; but so far as their effect upon us individually is concerned, they do not become real to us until we give them life with our own thinking or through the workings of our imaginations.

This may appear a little strange at first reading, but it will perhaps become clearer if I cite a few examples. For instance, you are advised to wear rubbers when you go out in the rain. We've all heard the remark, "If you don't, you'll catch your death of cold." That thought has never had the slightest effect upon me. I haven't worn rubbers since I was a small child. I have had my shoes and feet thoroughly wet hundreds of times, often for hours at a time, yet I cannot recall ever having caught cold as a result. Some people have a tremendous fear of drafts, but I have often thought that if they did catch cold by being in a draft, it was because of their fearful thoughts rather than because of the drafts themselves. I sit in drafts for long periods daily, and at night I sleep in a corner room which has windows on two sides. I raise them in all sorts of weather, so that the wind often sweeps across me. Yet I've never had a cold as a result, because I never give it a thought.

However, I do not advise anyone accustomed to wearing rubbers to go without them; neither do I suggest to anyone afraid of drafts to stay in them—because lifelong habits and beliefs with their consequences are not going to change overnight.

For centuries, outstanding thinkers have claimed that man could shape events and control matter through his mind alone, and the more you study this science, the more you will realize the amazing powers of your own mind.

Sir Arthur Conan Doyle, creator of Sherlock Holmes and for many years a member of the British Society for Psychic Research, declared that in thought alone there was a constructive and destructive power akin to the "faith that can move mountains." He said that while the results themselves were conclusive, he had no idea what power it was that came from a man's mind and that could separate the molecules of a solid object toward which it was directed. I know that materialists will scoff at such a statement. But just remember how radio waves pass right through wood, brick, steel, and other so-called solid objects. If thought waves, or whatever they are, can be tuned to even higher oscillations, why can't they affect the molecules of solid objects?

There are many professional gamblers who contend that a strong mental influence has much to do with achieving so-called lucky results in such games of chance as card playing, dice, roulette, etc. I know one man who was able to step up to an old-fashioned cigar store punchboard and with a few punches grab off the best prizes. Once I asked him about it, and he said, "I never go near a punchboard unless I am in the mood for it, and that means that I must be in the frame of mind that I'm going to win. I've noticed that if there's the slightest doubt in my mind, I don't win. But I can't recall the time that I didn't get winning numbers when the winning idea was firmly fixed in my mind before I started to play."

At Duke University, Dr. J. B. Rhine and his associates demonstrated that psychokinesis, the name given to designate the mind's power to influence material objects, is much more than idle theory. Dice (yes, the regular old dice used in crap games) were thrown by a mechanical device to eliminate all possibility of personal influence and trickery. Experiments of this type were started in 1934, and there were many tests in which millions of throws of the dice were made. The results were such that Dr. Rhine declared, "There is no better explanation than the subjects influenced the fall of the dice without any recognized physical contacts with them." By mentally concentrating upon the appearance of certain numbers, while standing at a distance to avoid all physical contact with the mechanical thrower and with the dice, the experimenters were frequently able to control the way the dice landed. In a number of the experiments, the scores refuted some of the traditional mathematical odds of millions to one against the reappearance of certain combinations of numbers in repeated succession. (For more on Dr. Rhine's work, see Chapter Seven.)

Meditate over this for a few minutes and realize what it means to you. Those experiments give you some idea of what is meant by "Thought creates after its kind," "Thought correlates with its object," "Thought attracts that upon which it is directed," and similar statements that metaphysicians have been claiming for years. It was Job who said, "For the thing which I greatly feared is come upon me." Our fearful thoughts are just as creative and magnetic in attracting troubles to us as are the constructive and positive thoughts in attracting welcome results. So no matter what the character of your thoughts, they do create after their kind. When this sinks into your consciousness, you get some inkling of the awe-inspiring power which is yours to use.

While thoughts do create and exercise control far beyond any limits yet known to man, I cling to the theory that they create only according to their pitch, intensity, emotional quality, depth of feeling, or vibratory plane. In other words, thoughts have a creative or controlling force in the exact ratio of their constancy, intensity, and power—comparable to the wave length and wattage of a broadcasting station.

While many explanations have been offered, it is fairly certain that thought is not a form of electrical energy, but something else yet to be defined. In a series of telepathy experiments, subjects were placed in a Faraday Cage, which effectively blocked any possible transmission of electrical energy. Yet the subjects' scores were still well above chance: whatever was carrying data from one mind to another, it was clearly not electrical. Nevertheless, I have done a great deal of experiments with high-frequency electricity, the field in which the great electrical genius Nikola Tesla pioneered. And so, whenever I think of thought and its radiations or vibrations, I instinctively link them up with electricity and its phenomena. In this manner they become more understandable to me.

I find that I am far from being alone in holding this analogy. Nowadays, practically every hospital is equipped with an EEG, or electro-encephalograph—an apparatus that detects and records a patient's brain waves. These "waves" are, in effect, the electrical oscillations of the brain's two hemispheres. Doctors use them to diagnose not only the health of the brain and nervous system, but as clues to a patient's general mental health, to his or her dreams and emotional state, and even to the existence of disease elsewhere in the body.

In 1944, Dr. Harold S. Burr and his co-workers at Yale University, after experimenting for twelve years, reached the conclusion that all living things are surrounded by an electrical aura of their own making, and that life is connected electrically to the whole pattern of the universe. For years, mystics, occultists, and metaphysicians have claimed that each individual possesses such an aura, and there are countless cases in which these auras have been recorded as actually seen.

Then in the late 1960s, Soviet researchers announced the discovery of Kirlian photography: a technique for capturing the "aura" on photographic film. Kirlian photos of a leaf showed it to be a galaxy of bright sparkles—which, however, slowly dimmed as the leaf wilted. Kirlian photographs of subjects' hands showed bright rays emanating from the fingers—which seemed to confirm the metaphysicians' age-old belief that one's hands are a source of healing energy. Critics objected that the Kirlian process was recording nothing more than an electrical coronal discharge, generated by the mild electrical field in which the photographs were taken. Yet at the same time, it was clear that the strength of the Kirlian "aura" *does* correlate with the subject's emotional state. A number of psychologists—notably Dr. Lee R. Steiner of New York—found this correlation so reliable that they used Kirlian photography as an objective measure of their patients' progress.

We can reconcile this apparent paradox if we look at electricity, coronal discharges, and the Kirlian effect as *byproducts* of that yet-to-be-identified thought energy, just as tidal waves in the ocean are visible "translations" of earthquakes that may have taken place hundreds of miles away on the sea floor.

Hermes Trismegistus and the ancient Hermetic philosophers all taught the theory of vibration. Pythagoras, the great geometrician and philosopher who lived in the sixth century before Christ, held that everything that exists is a vibration. This is the very essence of our scientific electronic theory of today—that all matter consists of electrons (with a negative charge), nuetrons (with a neutral charge), protons (with a positive charge), and other sub-atomic particles, each with their own charges, which constantly act and react with one another.

For want of a better term, I use the word "vibration" or "oscillation": when the vibrations of its component molecules are speeded up, the form of a material object often changes—as when an ice cube melts in a hot skillet and soon evaporates into steam. But the essential differences in matter, and in the so-called elements as we know them, arise mainly from their differing numbers of electrons, neutrons, and protons. By adding and subtracting protons, nuclear scientists can actually change atoms of one element into atoms of another—thus verifying the ancient alchemists' claim that lesser elements, such as iron and lead, could be transmuted into silver and gold. The alchemists also were able to heal all disease by the same forces.

When you realize that your nervous system is reached only through vibration—in other words, that our five known senses record vision, hearing, touch, taste, and smell by means of vibrations given off by the external things themselves—you get a better understanding of the nature of vibrations. For example, we hear a loud noise. It comes to us only via the sound vibration through the air. We see a green leaf, but it is merely a pattern of light waves as gathered by the eyes and transmitted to the brain. There are, however, many vibrations pitched at a much greater frequency than our senses are attuned to, and of which we never have any conscious knowledge. For example, there is a whistle pitched so high that only a dog can hear it.

We have all heard of the power of "the laying on of hands," and most of us know how soothing hands stroking our temples can lessen the intensity of a headache. Can this be due to some form of energy flowing from our finger ends? The Bible tells of numerous instances where healing was accomplished by the touch of Jesus's hand. Does the explanation lie in this little-known field of electricity—the science of vibration? And does this electrical atmosphere, which Dr. Burr claims is of our own making and which surrounds all living things, enable us to cause certain impulses to pour forth literally from our fingers or from our minds—vibratory forces that can act upon others and upon so-called material objects? In the wintertime, and at high altitudes, you can feel and often see the electric spark that results from walking across the rug and then touching some metallic object. That, of course, is a form of static electricity generated by friction, but it gives an idea of how one kind of electricity can be developed through the body.

Among pictures descriptive of the experiments of Yale investigators is one showing that when subjects dipped their forefingers in saltwater cups connected with a galvanometer, there was a flow of electricity between the positive left hand and the negative right hand, measuring 1.5 millivolts. In another picture, two middle fingers, one with a slight cut at the tip, were partially immersed in the cups. But this time the polarity of the hands changed, the left hand changing from positive to negative and the right becoming positive, with the current stepping up to 12 millivolts.

As I looked at those pictures, I recalled an instrument perfected many years ago by a French scientist, Dr. Hippolyte Baraduc. Known as a "biometre," it consisted of a bell-shaped glass in which was suspended a cooper needle fastened to a fine silk thread. Below the needle, but inside the glass, was a circular piece of cardboard marked off into degrees.

Two of these instruments were placed side by side, and the operator held the fingers of both hands within half an inch of the glass, his mind concentrated on the delicately balanced needle. By changing his mental attitude or the polarity of his thinking, the operator could cause corresponding changes in the direction of the needle, now in one direction and now in another, the needle following his changing thought currents.

Here is a simple experiment embodying similar principles. Take a piece of medium-weight paper, about three inches square, and fold it diagonally from corner to corner. Then open it and make another diagonal fold so that there are two folds or creases forming intersecting diagonals. Again open the paper, which will now present the appearance of a low, partially flattened-out pyramid. Now take a long needle and force it through a cork so that the point extends an inch or so above the top of the cork. Place the cork with its needle, point up, on an inverted water glass, so that there may be free movement of the paper which is to revolve on the needle point. Then take the piece of paper and place the spot where the creases intersect on the point of the needle, with the four sides of the pyramid sloping downward.

Place the glass, with the cork, needle, and paper on a table or desk in a room free from drafts. Keep away from heat registers or windows, thus avoiding possible heat waves or air currents. Then place your hands around the piece of paper in a semi-cupped position, keeping the fingers a half inch or so away, so that the paper may revolve freely. Now order it to revolve upon the needle point.

At first it will wobble—perhaps revolving slowly at first and in one direction or the other; but if your hands remain steady and you concentrate upon a certain direction of movement, the paper will revolve until it turns rapidly upon the needle point. If you mentally order a change in direction, the one-way movement will cease and the paper will start revolving in the opposite direction. Of course, it is essential that you do not breathe or exhale in the direction of the paper.

Many explanations of what causes the paper to revolve have been offered—heat waves from the hands, a body reflex of some kind, and the like. If the paper revolved in only one direction, then one of these explanations could be possible. But when a person, with a little practice and confident and concentrated thinking, can cause the paper to revolve first in one direction and then in another by reversing the polarity of his thinking, it is clear that the principle is the same as that which governs experiments with the biometre.

Another similar experiment uses a dialette, a small disc of cardboard bearing the facsimile of the face of a clock, with numbers from one to twelve. (This is better known as the Rosicrucian Dialette and is issued by Amorc, Rosicrucian Brotherhood.) A sharp needle is pushed through its center and on top of the needle is balanced a sliver of thin cardboard in the shape of an arrow. The disc is placed on top of a glass filled with water in which the lower part of the needle is submerged. The operator places his hands around the top of the glass, the disc, and arrow; then orders the arrow to revolve, change its position, or stop at any desired position or number. However, not everyone can immediately get satisfactory results in these experiments, because the power of mind, thought concentration, and projective influence vary from individual to individual.

If a form of electricity emanates from our hands or fingers in particular and if waves, either dynamic or magnetic vibrations, are set up by our thinking, we then have an explanation of table-tipping, automatic writing, the performances of the planchette or Ouija board, and many other mediumistic and occult operations. Dr. Phillips Thomas, research engineer for the Westinghouse Electric Company, in 1937, told the Utah session of the American Electric Institute, "We feel certain that whatever we do, say, or think is accomplished by some type of radiation. We think such radiations are electricity. In the near future, we may be able to capture and interpret these radiations of personality and thought through electrical impulses."

Since some of my readers may not have a clear understanding

of the radiation of thought, I offer a simple explanation. A pebble tossed into a pond immediately sets up a series of ripples or small waves, which spread out circle-like on the surface of the water and ultimately reach the shoreline, where they appear to stop. The larger the pebble, the higher the waves. Two stones of different sizes and weights, tossed in simultaneously at different places but in close proximity, will each set up a series of waves, converging upon each other. Where the two sets meet, there appears to be a struggle as to which is to overcome or pass the other. As far as our physical vision is concerned, if the waves are of the same size, both seem to stop or merge at their meeting-point; but if one is larger than the other, it sweeps over the smaller and creates waves in the wake of the smaller ripples.

Think about this in connection with your own mental impulses—for example, how thoughts of one nature stop or over-whelm others. You can readily appreciate that the more powerful or concentrated the thought, the quicker its tempo, the greater its vibration, the more it sweeps aside weaker vibrations and the more rapidly it does its creative work.

We hear much about various stages of meditation, levels of consciousness, thought concentration, the strength of our faith—all of which deals with the intensity or degree of power we send forth. Creative force comes only when a thought is completely rounded-out, when the imagination can visualize the fulfillment of your ambition and see in your mind a picture of the object you desire—a house, a car, a television—just as if you already possessed them.

After studying the so-called mystic teachings, the various mental sciences, and the regular church teachings, I am convinced that they all work in varying degrees, but only to the extent that their followers believe. So it is with prayer, whether it be a part of a church service or the purely spontaneous and personal supplication of the individual.

However, I am forced to conclude that many people go through the lip-service of saying their prayers without the slightest belief that those prayers will be answered. Consequently, they are not answered. I am frequently reminded of the story of the old lady, professing a belief in prayer, who planned to go shopping. The day before, she prayed that the sun would shine on her shopping day.

Upon completion of her prayer she glanced out of the window, saw some black clouds, and instantly declared, "But I know it's going to rain."

In the late fall of 1944, an article by Thomas Sugrue in the *Saturday Review of Literature* declared that the mind-cure movement had grown so rapidly that it was now encountered everywhere. He cited several cases in which sufferers had secured phenomenal results. One woman, who at sixty-two had been partially crippled, her fingers bent with arthritis, had taken up a system of Yogi breathing and had entirely recovered from her physical ailments. Mr. Sugrue declared that after her restoration to health, those who saw her judged her to be about forty. Another woman achieved excellent results under an occult system of metaphysics, and guesses as to her age were fifteen years under her real age. Sugrue told also of a retired missionary who for the past twelve years had experimented with psychic phenomena and had obtained most startling results.

We can come to only one conclusion: that is that all the systems, creeds, and cults work as a result of the firm beliefs of the individual—and that brings us to the magic of believing.

Sigmund Freud, the founder of psychoanalysis, brought forth the hypothesis that a powerful force within us, an unilluminated part of the mind—separate from the conscious mind—is constantly at work molding our thoughts, feelings, and actions. It isn't an organ of so-called physical matter, such as we know the brain to be, and science hasn't located its tangible position in the human body. Nevertheless, it is there, and from the beginning of recorded time, man has known that it exists. The ancients often referred to it as the "spirit." Paracelsus called it the will, others have called it the mind, an adjunct of the brain. Some have referred to it as conscience, the creator of the "still, small voice within." Others have called this division of our mental existence the soul, and some metaphysical teachers claim that it is located in the solar plexus. Others call it the super-ego, the inner power, the super-consciousness, the unconscious, the subconscious, and various other names. Still others have asserted that it is a part of the Supreme Intelligence to which we are all linked. Hence the name Universal Mind—that which embraces every living thing, all human as well as plant and animal life.

No matter what we call it—I prefer the term *subconscious*—it is recognized as the essence of life, and the limits of its power are unknown. It never sleeps. It comes to our support in times of great trouble, it warns us of impending danger, it often aids us to do what seems impossible. It guides us in many ways and when properly employed, performs so-called miracles.

Objectively, it does as it is told—that is, when it is commanded or besought by the conscious mind; subjectively, it acts primarily upon its own initiative, although there are times when its activity appears to be the result of influences from the outside.

Sir Arthur Eddington is quoted as saying, "I believe that the mind has the power to affect groups of atoms and even tamper with the odds of atomic behavior, and that even the course of the world is not predetermined by physical laws but may be altered by the uncaused volition of human beings."

When this idea is fully comprehended, it becomes breath-taking. It is more understandable in the light of the electronic or vibratory theory.

Every student of the subject knows what may be accomplished by getting into direct contact with the subconscious mind—thousands have employed it to achieve wealth, power, and fame in this world, as well as to cure physical ailments and solve countless human problems. And its power is there for you to use. The only steps you have to take are to believe in its power and use the technique set forth in this book—or else devise a system of your own that will put it to work for you.

Dana Sleeth's syndicated column covering the observations of a hillbilly was well known to newspaper readers in the 1920s. He once told me that he considered the subconscious mind one of his greatest aids, not only in furnishing him with ideas but in helping him find lost tools and other articles. Mr. Sleeth at the time was living in the hills, remote from cities and towns, alternating as a columnist and farmer. He had made an extensive study of the subject, and we often discussed it in letters covering our ideas.

It's a wonderful thing—the subconscious mind, [said Mr. Sleeth], and for the life of me I can't see why more people don't learn about it and its use. I don't know how many thousands of times it has helped me with my problems.

Ideas for feature stories have often come to me when I was engaged in such lowly tasks as stump grubbing. And as for locating lost tools—it's a knockout.

You know nothing is ever lost—it's just misplaced. It's right there to be found in the exact place where you left it or dropped it. I have found dozens of misplaced tools in the identical spot where my subconscious mind told me to look. Say, for example, it was a pocket knife—mine's a good-sized one—that I had misplaced or dropped. I would say, "Pocket knife, where are you?" Then I would close my eyes for a moment, or I might gaze off into space—the answer might not always come immediately, but when it did, it would come in a flash, and I would be led right to the spot where lay the knife. It always seemed to work unfailingly—even to such things as axes, rakes, and other tools that I was constantly leaving around somewhere—you know we newspaper people are not very methodical.

I used to have a great deal of difficulty in remembering names, but I have found that if I could visualize the man or woman whose name I had temporarily forgotten, and see an outline of his or her features, the color of the eyes, hair, manner of dress, etc., the subconscious would bring me the name without difficulty.

I don't know where I learned this, but in trying to recall something, a certain story or certain fact that appeared at the moment to escape me, I would relax, elevate my head and put my right hand a couple of inches above my forehead. Sometimes I might close my eyes or gaze off into space; but this little trick always seemed to get results.

Never forget: inventions, great musical compositions, poetry, fiction, and all other ideas for original accomplishment come from the subconscious. Give it the thought or the material and keep it going with a deep-rooted desire for performance, and you will get results. There is an old saying that once we start weaving, the Gods will furnish the skein, and how true that is!

When you start to operate with the aid of this power, the bricks automatically fall into place as though a magical hand had touched them. Results will certainly follow in a most astounding manner. Ideas for accomplishment will pop here and they will pop there.

What may appear as coincidences are not coincidences at all, but simply the working out of the pattern which you started with your own weaving.

I am certain that thousands of successful men and women reach great heights and accomplish marvelous results without knowing anything about the subconscious mind and with no knowledge that it was the power which made for accomplishments.

Living here in the hills away from people and everyday influences, I have often felt that those who live close to nature were in a much better position to utilize the subconscious than others. I believe that day will come when science will prove that the great power of the subconscious is one of the most formidable forces in shaping and controlling our lives.

A passing, momentary thought-flicker dies almost a-borning, although it may later reveal cumulative power. But the force that brings into play the great system of the subconscious is a sustained thought—or, as I mentioned before, a fixed mental picture. In order to bring subconscious forces into action, there are many methods for stepping up the tempo of the vibrations of conscious thought although some times, just a single utterance, a momentary glance and a word or two traveling from one person to another, will bring the subconscious into immediate action. So it is with catastrophic danger, moments of great peril and periods of great stress, which suddenly confront a person with the necessity for immediate action. The subconscious comes to the aid of those in the habit of making quick decisions almost instantaneously, and it comes into operation when you have cleared your conscious mind of its multitude of conflicting thoughts. "Going into the silence" is another way of expressing it. Don Juan told Carlos Castaneda that the mind's constant chatter was a major barrier to getting in touch with any higher guidance.

Perhaps the most effective method of bringing the subconscious into practical play is through making mental pictures. Use your imagination to perfect an image of the thing or situation as you would like it to exist in physical form. This is usually referred to as visualization.

However, most sustained and continuing manifestations come as a result of deep-seated belief. Through this belief, with its strange power, miracles happen and peculiar phenomena occur for which there appears to be no known explanation. I refer now to unquestioning belief—a firm and positive conviction that goes through every fiber of your being—when you believe with your heart and soul.

Call it a phase of emotion, a spiritual force, a type of electrical vibration—anything you please—but that's the force that brings outstanding results, sets the law of attraction into operation, and allows sustained thought to correlate with its object. Belief changes the tempo of the mind or thought-frequency. Like a huge magnet, it draws the subconsious forces into play, changing your whole aura and affecting everything about you—including people and objects at great distances. It often brings into your individual sphere of life results that are sometimes startling—results you never dreamed possible.

Countless references to belief appear in the Bible. It is the first condition for membership in many religious, fraternal, and political organizations. Leaders everywhere are looking for people who have the kinds of beliefs they will fight for, because the people charged with the vibrations of strong beliefs sometimes do the miraculous, things others often say are unbelievable. That kind of belief has the magic touch. Indeed, it is the basic principle in both white and black magic.

chapter three

What the subconscious really is

No artist, man of science, or writer of any distinction, however little disposed to self-analysis, is not aware by personal experience of the unequalled importance of the subconscious," wrote Gustave Geley, distinguished French psychologist and author of *From the Unconscious to the Conscious.* He pointed out that up to the nineteenth century, the psychology of the subconscious was completely ignored, and was considered only as the cause of abnormal disease or accident. Geley added that the best results in life were obtained by close harmony and cooperation between the conscious and subconscious minds.

The subconscious plays a very important part in the magic of believing. It will bring you a quicker understanding of this science. You will have a clear and detailed picture of what the subconscious mind is, where it is located, and how it functions—both by itself, and in collaboration with the conscious mind. Some of the material in this chapter you will find referred to or repeated in later chapters. But remember that repetition is an essential part of the technique of this science. Repetition is equally effective in presenting the knowledge of this science. Furthermore, the faster you get an understanding of it, the quicker you will be on your way to getting whatever you desire.

In giving you this picture of the subconscious mind, I must use scientific terms here and there, since practically all the knowledge of the subconscious has come from the study and experimentation of some of the world's greatest psychologists. But even if you find this a little difficult to understand at first, repeated readings will make it all clear, giving you a solid foundation upon which to proceed with the active part of the science.

As I told you in the first chapter, *The Law of Psychic Phenomena* by Thomson Jay Hudson first got me thinking about the subconscious mind and its great possibilities for helping individuals in everyday life. Since that time, other books—such as *The Sub-Conscious Speaks* by Erna Ferrell Grabe and Paul C. Ferrell, *The Source of Power* by Theodore Clinton Foote, *The Unconscious* by Morton Prince, M.D., and *Common Sense and Its Cultivation* by Hanbury Hankin—have greatly added to the knowledge of the subject. I intend to give you a picture of the conscious and subconscious minds, as well as definite instructions as to how you can bring them under control and direct their energies toward fulfilling your desires.

"There is dormant in each human being a faculty, whether developed or not, which will enable that particular individual to succeed if the *desire for success* is present in his conscious mind." Thus wrote the authors of *The Sub-Conscious Speaks*. This "faculty" has always been known and recognized for its strange and unusual powers, but not until about a century and a half ago did psychologists who made it the subject of their special investigation and experimentation, call it the subconscious mind. Emerson was certainly aware of the dual character of the human mental organization when he wrote in his *Journals*, "I find one state of mind does not remember or conceive of another state. Thus I have written within a twelve-month verses ['Days'] which I do not remember the composition or correction of, and could not write the like today, and have only for proof of their being mine, various external evidences, as the MS. in which I find them, and the circumstances that I have sent copies of them to friends, etc., etc."

Today the words conscious and subconscious are widely

understood. It is recognized that we all have two minds, each one endowed with separate and distinct attributes and powers, and each one capable, under certain conditions, of independent action. There is no difficulty in comprehending that the conscious mind operates in the brain, for whenever you do any concentrated thinking, you feel it in your head. Sometimes the thought is so intense and prolonged that your head aches, or your eyes become tired, or your temples throb. Also, you can generally trace the source of the thought. It may be suggested by something you have seen or heard or read; perhaps it is a new idea for your business or home; maybe it is the continuation of some thought you have been pondering for a long time—in short, you can connect it with something already related to your consciousness. Sometimes your thought is concerned with trying to solve a difficult problem, and you have become so exhausted and discouraged at failing to arrive at a solution that you "give it up," "let the whole thing go," "dismiss it from your mind," an action you often take at night when you can't sleep because of the thought that is pounding and gripping your brain. The moment you let it go, it begins to sink, as though it were moving downward somewhere inside of you. The tension in your conscious mind then decreases and you are soon asleep. The next morning when you wake up, your conscious mind begins to think again about the problem, when suddenly there appears before your mind's eyes a mental picture of the complete solution, with all the necessary directions for appropriate action on your part.

When you released it from your conscious mind, where did the thought go? Through what power inside of you was the problem solved? Many writers, orators, artists, musical composers, designers, inventors, and other creative workers have long made use of their subconscious minds, either consciously or unconsciously. Merton S. Yewdale, well-known book editor, called my attention to a statement by the American novelist Louis Bromfield:

> *One of the most helpful discoveries I made long ago in common with some other writers is that there is a part of the mind, which the psychologists call the "subconscious" that works while you are sleeping or even while you are relaxing or engaged in some other task far removed from writing. I have found it possible to train this part of the mind to do a pretty organized job. Very often I have awakened in the morning to find a problem of technique, or plot, or*

character, which had long been troubling me, completely solved while I had been sleeping. The judgment of the "subconscious mind" which represents inherited instincts and the accumulation of experience, is virtually infallible, and I would always trust its decisions over any judgment arrived at through a long and reasonable process of conscious thinking.

No doubt you already have a mental picture of your two minds: the conscious mind in your head, above the line of consciousness; and the subconscious mind in your body, below the line of consciousness—with a means of communication between them.

Now the conscious mind is the source of thought. Also, it gives us the sense of awareness in our normal waking life; the knowledge that we are ourselves here and now; the recognition and understanding of our environment; the power to rule over our mental faculties, to recall the events of our past life, and to comprehend our emotions and their significance. More concretely, it enables us to have a rational understanding of the objects and persons about us, of our own successes or shortcomings, of the validity of an argument, or the beauty of a work of art.

The chief powers of the conscious mind are reason, logic, form, judgment, calculation, conscience, and the moral sense. By it we take cognizance of the object world, and its means of observation are our five physical senses. Our conscious mind is the outgrowth of our physical necessities, and likewise our guide in the struggle with our material environment. Its highest function is that of reasoning, and by all methods—inductive and deductive, analytic and synthetic. For example, suppose you are undertaking to discover a new theory. You use your conscious mind and employ the inductive method of reasoning. That is, you first collect the facts and elements presented to your sense perceptions; then you compare them one with another, noting similarities and dissimilarities. Then you select those which are alike in qualities, in uses, or in function, after which you proceed to form a generalization or law, that certain things which have such qualities will function in such a way.

This is the scientific method of arriving at knowledge, and it forms the basis of modern education in schools and colleges. We all use it in some form or other, to help solve our problems, whether personal, social, business, professional, or economic. Many times the solution of our problems results from this use of our conscious mind. But now and then, when the solution is not forthcoming, we become exhausted with continued trying. We begin to lose confidence in ourselves, and we often resign ourselves to the idea that we have failed and that nothing can be done about it. Here is where the subconscious mind comes in—to help renew our belief in ourselves, to assist us to overcome our difficulty, and to put us on the road to achievement and success.

Just as the conscious mind is the source of thought, so the subconscious is the source of power. Rooted in instinct, it is aware of the individual's most elemental desires, and it is always pressing upward into conscious existence. It is a repository of spontaneous impressions of men and nature, and a memory vault in which are kept the records of facts and experiences sent down to it from time to time by the conscious mind for safekeeping and future use. Thus the subconscious mind is not only a mighty storehouse of ever-ready material that can be placed at the disposal of the conscious mind, but also a powerhouse of energy with which the individual can be charged, thus enabling him to recover his strength, courage, and faith in himself. Such is the power of your subconscious mind.

The subconscious mind is beyond space and time, and is fundamentally a powerful sending and receiving station with a universal hookup. It can communicate with the physical, mental, psychic, and—according to many investigators—spiritual worlds. In brief, the subconscious embodies the feeling and wisdom of the past, the awareness and knowledge of the present, and the thought and vision of the future. Emerson, though he wrote of "instinct," endowed it with so many superior attributes that he undoubtedly was thinking of the subconscious mind when he wrote, "All true wisdom of thought and of action comes of deference to this instinct, patience with its delays. To make a practical use of this instinct in every part of life constitutes true wisdom, and we must form the habit of preferring in all cases its guidance, which is given as it is used."

The powers of the subconscious are many: intuition, emotion, certitude, inspiration, suggestion, deduction, imagination, organization, and, of course, memory and dynamic energy. It takes cognizance of its environment by means independent of the physical senses. It perceives by intuition. It operates most successfully and performs its highest function when the objective senses are quiescent. But it can function during the waking hours as well as during sleep. As a distinct entity, it possesses independent powers and functions, with a unique mental organization all its own. It sustains an existence closely allied to the physical body and the life of the individual, yet also operates independently of the body.

Now the subconscious mind has three primary functions. First, with its intuitive understanding of the bodily needs, it maintains and preserves (unaided by the conscious mind) the well-being and indeed the very life of the physical body. Second, as pointed out in the last chapter, in times of great emergency it springs into immediate action (again independently of the conscious mind) and takes supreme command, acting with incredible certitude, rapidity, accuracy, and understanding. Third, it is operative in the psychic world. The psychic powers of the subconscious are manifested in such phenomena as telepathy, clairvoyance, and psychokinesis. But, also, it can be summoned to help the conscious mind in time of great personal necessity, when the conscious calls upon the subconscious to use its powers and resources to solve a vital problem or bring to pass whatever the individual seeks or desires. In this book we are concerned particularly with the technique by which the subconscious mind operates for your benefit.

Accordingly, to draw upon the resources and powers of the subconscious and awaken it into action, you must first be sure you are asking for something that is rightfully yours to have and within your ability to handle, for the subconscious manifests itself only according to a person's capabilities. Next, in conveying your need to the subconscious, it must be in images of the work having *already been done*. Thus, while it is necessary for you to *feel* and *think* yourself successful, it is important to go one step further and actually *see* yourself as already successful, either in the performance of some selected task or as actually occupying the position to which you aspire. For the next and final step, you must wait patiently while the subconscious assimilates the elements of your problem and then goes about its own way to work it out for you. You must have patience and absolute faith, for, as Theodore Simon Jouffroy, the French philosopher, said, "The subconscious mind will not take the trouble to work for those who do not *believe* in it."

In due course, with the flowing of the ideas and plans of the subconscious into your waiting conscious mind, the solution of your problem will be revealed to you and the correct course of action indicated. You must receive the message from the subconscious freely, and after understanding it you must act at once, immediately and unquestioningly. There must be no hesitation on your part, no mental reservation, no deliberation. Only by a prompt and automatic response will you make your subconscious continue to respond whenever you call upon it.

However, your problem may be one that cannot be solved in this manner. Instead of receiving the solution in the form of a "blueprint" to guide your steps to the final fulfillment, at intervals you may feel some mysterious force urging you to do certain things that seem to have no special significance or logical connection. Nevertheless, you must continue to believe in the power and wisdom of the subconscious. Obediently perform the seemingly irrelevant things, and one day you will find yourself in the position you sought, doing the work you envisioned for yourself. Then, when you look back, you will see how the things you were called upon to do, through the aid of the subconscious, all formed a logical line of events, the last one of which was your final arriving—the reward of your sincerest hopes and desires, your own triumphant personal success!

chapter four

Suggestion is power

How many times have you heard it said, "Just believe you can do it and you can"? Whatever the task, if begun with the belief that you can do it, it will be done perfectly. Often belief empowers a person to do what others consider impossible. The *act* of believing is the starting force, the generating power that leads to accomplishment.

"Come on, fellows, we can beat them," shouts someone in command, whether in a football game, on the battlefield, or in the strife of the business world. That sudden voicing of belief, challenging and electrifying, reverses the tide and—Success! From defeat to victory—and all because some mighty believer knew that *it could be done.*

You may be shipwrecked and tossed into the water near a rocky shore. Momentarily, you may fear that there isn't a chance for you. Suddenly a feeling comes that you *will* be saved—or that you can save yourself. The moment you have that feeling, it begins to take the form of belief. And along with the belief comes the power to assist you.

You may be in a fire, surrounded by flames and enveloped in

smoke, and frantic with fear. This same power asserts itself—and you may be saved. Emerson explains it by saying that in a difficult situation or a sudden emergency, our spontaneous action is always the best. Many stories have been told of the great reserves of the subconscious mind, how under its direction (and by imparting its superhuman strength), frail men and women have been able to perform feats far beyond their normal powers. Speakers, stand-up comedians, and writers are often amazed at the subconscious mind's power to furnish them with a steady flow of thoughts that their audiences enjoy.

After studying the various mystical religions and different teachings and systems of mind-stuff, I'm impressed that they all have the same basic *modus operandi*. That is, they achieve success through repetition—the repeating of certain mantras, words, or formulas. William Seabrook declared that witch doctors, Voodoo high priests, "hexers," and many other followers of strange cults use just plain mumbo-jumbo to invoke the spirits or work black magic. One finds the same principle at work in the chants, incantations, litanies, daily lessons (to be repeated at frequently as possible during the week), and the frequent praying of the Buddhists and Moslems alike. Or consider the affirmations of the Theosophists and the followers of Unity, the Absolute, Truth, New Thought, Divine Science. In fact, it is basic in all religions, although here it is white magic instead of black. When you seek further, you find the same principle at work in the beating of tom-toms or kettledrums by primitive peoples in all parts of the globe. The sound vibrations arouse similar vibrations in the psychic nature of these so-called "primitives," so that they become stimulated, excited, and emotionalized to the point where they can defy death. The war dances of the American Indians, with their repeated rhythmic physical movements; the tribal ceremonies to bring rain; the dancing of the whirling dervishes—even the playing of martial music at critical times, and the soothing background music played for the workers in industrial plants—all embody the same principle.

In his book, *Penthouse of the Gods*, published in 1939, Theos Bernard recounts some interesting facts as to the repetition of certain mystical chants and prayers. When he wrote it, he claimed to be the first white person to enter the mysterious Tibetan city of Lhasa, high in the Himalayas, where the monasteries contained thousands of lamas—followers of Buddha. On reading the book, you get the impression that when the lamas and monks are not eating or attending to the material wants of their bodies, they are constantly and continuously engaged in their mystical chants, using their prayer wheels. Bernard declared that in one temple, the monks started at daybreak and spent the entire day repeating prayers. The exact number of their repetitions was 108,000. He told also of how lamas accompanying him repeated certain fixed chants in order to give him additional strength.

In all religions, cults, and orders, there is an obvious, prescribed ritual in which the repetition of words (mystical or otherwise) plays an important part. And this brings us to the law of suggestion. Forces operating within its limits are capable of producing phenomenal results. That is, the power of suggestion—either autosuggestion (your own to yourself) or heterosuggestion (coming to you from outside sources)—starts the machinery into operation, causing the subconscious mind to begin its creative work—and right here is where the affirmations and repetitions play their part. Repetition of the same chant, the same incantations, the same affirmations leads to belief, and once that belief becomes a deep conviction, things begin to happen. A builder or contractor looks over a set of plans and specifications for a bridge or a building, and, urged by a desire to get the contract for the work, declares to himself, "I can do that. Yes, I can do that." He may repeat it silently to himself a thousand times without being conscious of doing it. Nevertheless, the suggestion finds a place in which to take root, he gets the contract, and the structure is eventually built. Conversely, he may say that he can't do it—and he never does.

Hitler used the identical force and the same mechanics in inciting the German people to attack the world. A reading of his *Mein Kampf* will verify that. Dr. René Fauvel, a famous French psychologist, explained it by saying that Hitler had a remarkable understanding of the law of suggestion and its different forms of application, and that he mobilized every instrument of propaganda in his mighty campaign of suggestion with uncanny skill and masterly showmanship. Hilter openly stated that the psychology of suggestion was a terrible weapon in the hands of anyone who knew how to use it.

Let's see how he worked it to make the Germans believe what he wanted them to. Slogans, posters, huge signs, massed flags appeared throughout Germany. Hitler's picture was everywhere. "One Reich, one People, one Leader" became the chant. It was heard everywhere that a group gathered. "Today we own Germany, tomorrow the entire world," the marching song of the German youths, came from thousands of throats daily. Such slogans as "Germany has waited long enough," "Stand up, you are the aristocrats of the Third Reich," "Germany is behind Hitler to a man," and hundreds of others, bombarded them twenty-four hours a day from billboards, sides of buildings, the radio, and the press. Every time they moved, turned around, or spoke to one another, they got the idea that they were a superior race, and once that belief took hold, they started their campaign of terror. Under the hypnotic influence of this belief, strengthened by repeated suggestion, they started out to prove it. Unfortunately for them, other nations also had strong national beliefs that eventually became the means of bringing defeat to the Germans.

Mussolini, too, used the same law of suggestion in an attempt to give Italy a place in the sun. Signs and slogans such as "Believe, Obey, Fight," "Italy must have its great place in the world," "We have some old scores and new scores to settle," covered the walls of thousands of buildings, and similar ideas were dinned into the people via the radio and every other means of direct communication.

Joseph Stalin, too, used the same science to build Russia into what she is today. In November, 1946, the Institute of Modern Hypnotism, recognizing that Stalin had been using the great power of the repeated suggestion in order to make the Russian people believe in their strength, named him as one of the ten persons with the "most hyponotic eyes in the world," and rated him as a "mass hypnotist."

The Japanese warlords used it to make fanatical fighters out of their people. From the very day of their birth, Japanese children were fed the suggestion that they were direct descendants of Heaven and destined to rule the world. They prayed it, chanted it, and believed it; but here again, it was used wrongly.

For forty-four years, ever since the Russo-Japanese war, the Japanese immortalized Naval Warrant Officer Magoshichi Sugino, one of Japan's early suicide fighters and greatest heroes. Thousands of statues were erected to his memory. In repeated song and story, young Nipponese were taught to believe that they could die in no more heroic manner than by following his example. Millions of them believed it, and during the war thousands of them did die as Kamekazi pilots. Yet Sugino, who was supposed to have gone to his death while scuttling a ship to bottle up the Russian fleet at Port Arthur, didn't die in battle! He was picked up by a Chinese boat. Upon learning that he was being lauded by his people as a great martyr, he decided to remain obscure and became an exile in Manchuria. Although he was alive and well, it continued to be dinned into the ears of young Nipponese that there was no greater heroic act than to die as Sugino had. This terrible, persistent and deeply founded belief, though based entirely on a fable, caused thousands of Japanese to throw away their lives during the war. Finally, Associated Press dispatches from Tokyo in November, 1946, told how he was discovered after many years and was being returned home.

We Americans, too, were subjected to the power of suggestion long before World War I. We got it again in a big way under the direction of General Hugh Johnson with his N.R.A. plan. In World War II, we were constantly told that Germany and Japan had to be defeated unconditionally. Under the constant repetition of the same thought, all individual thinking was paralyzed and the mass mind became grooved to a certain pattern—*win the war unconditionally*. As one writer so ably said, "In war, the voice of dissension becomes the voice of treason."

Again we see the terrific force of thought repetition—it is our master, and we do as we are ordered. This subtle force of the repeated suggestion overcomes our reason, acting directly on our emotions and our feelings, finally penetrating to the very depths of our subconscious minds. This is the basic principle of all successful advertising—the continued and repeated suggestion that first makes you believe, after which you are eager to buy. In recent years we have enjoyed a vitamin spree. Vitamins, minerals, and various "natural" and "organic" foods have come to us from all sides, and millions buy them, so potent is the repeated suggestion of their value.

For centuries tomatoes were looked upon as poisonous. People dared not eat them until some fearless person tried them and lived. Today millions of people eat tomatoes, not knowing that they were considered unfit for human consumption. Conversely, the lowly spinach nearly went into the garbage pail after the United States Government declared that it did not contain the food values attributed to it for decades. Millions believed this and refused to honor Popeye's favorite dish any longer.

Clearly, the founders of all great religious movements knew much about the power of the repeated suggestion and gained far-reaching results with it. Religious teachings have been hammered into us from birth, into our mothers and fathers before us and into their parents and their parents before them. There's certainly white magic in that kind of believing.

Such statements as "What we don't know won't hurt us" and "Ignorance is bliss" take on greater significance when you realize that only the things you become conscious of can harm or bother you. We have all heard the story of the man who didn't know it couldn't be done and went ahead and did it. Psychologists tell us that as babies we have only two fears: the fear of loud noises and the fear of falling. All of our other fears are passed on to us or develop as a result of our experiences; they come from what we are taught or what we hear and see. I like to think of men and women as staunch oak trees that can stand firm amid the many crosscurrents of thought that whirl around them. But far too many people are like saplings that, swayed by every little breeze, ultimately grow in the direction of some strong wind of thought that blows against them.

The Bible is filled with examples of the power of thought and suggestion. Read Genesis, Chapter 30, verses 36 to 43, and you'll learn that even Jacob knew their power. The Bible tells how he developed spotted and speckled cattle, sheep, and goats by placing rods from trees, partially stripping them of their bark so they would appear spotted and marked, in the watering troughs where the animals came to drink. As you may have guessed, the flocks conceived before the spotted rods and brought forth cattle, "ringstraked, speckled, and spotted." (And incidentally, Jacob waxed exceedingly rich.)

Moses, too, was a master at suggestion. For forty years he used it on the Israelites, and it took them to the promised land of milk and honey. David, following the suggestive forces operating on him, slew the mighty, heavily armed Goliath with a pebble from a slingshot.

Joan of Arc, the frail little Maid of Orléans, heard voices and under their suggestive influences became imbued with the idea that she had a mission to save France. She was able to transmit her indomitable spirit to the hearts of her soldiers and she defeated the superior forces of the English at Orléans.

William James, father of modern psychology in America, declared that often our faith in advance of a doubtful undertaking is the only thing that can assure its successful conclusion. Man's faith, according to James, acts on the powers above him as a claim and creates its own verification. In other words, the thought becomes literally father to the fact. For further illumination of faith and its power, I suggest that you read the General Epistle of James in the New Testament.

Actually everyone who has ever witnessed a football or baseball game has seen this power of suggestion at work. Knute Rockne, the famous coach at Notre Dame, knew the value of suggestion and used it repeatedly, but always suited his method of applying it to the temperament of the individual team. On one Saturday afternoon, Notre Dame was playing in a particularly grueling game, and at the end of the first half was trailing badly. The players were in their dressing room nervously awaiting Rockne's arrival. Finally the door opened, and Rockne came in slowly. His eyes swept inquiringly over the squad—"Oh, excuse me, I made a mistake. I thought these were the quarters of the Notre Dame team." The door closed, and Rockne was gone.

Puzzled and then stung with fury, the team went out for the second half—and won the game.

Other writers, too, have explained the psychological methods Rockne used and have told how Fielding Yost of Michigan, Dan

McGuin of Vanderbilt, Herbert Crisler of Princeton, and dozens of others used the "magic" of suggestion to arouse their teams to great emotional heights. Before the Rose Bowl game of 1934, the "wise" tipsters rated the Columbia team as underdogs. They hadn't counted on Coach Lou Little and his stirring talks to his players day after day. When the whistle blew for the end of the game, the Columbia men were the top dogs over the "superior" Stanford team.

In 1935, Gonzaga University beat powerful Washington State 13 to 6 in one of the biggest upset games ever seen in the West. Gonzaga was a non-conference team, while the Washington State team, because of its great record, was thought to be unbeatable. Newspapers at the time reported assistant coach Sam Dagley as having declared that Gonzaga played inspired football. He revealed that for half an hour before the game, Coach Mike Pecarovich played "over and over" a phonograph record of one of Rockne's most rousing pep talks.

Years ago, Mickey Cochrane of the Detroit Tigers literally drove a second-division-minded group of baseball players to the top of the American League by using the power of the repeated suggestion. I quote from a newsapper dispatch: "Day after day, through the hot, hard grind, [Cochrane] preached the gospel of victory, impressing on the Tigers the 'continued thought' that the team which wins must go forward."

You see the same force actively at work in the fluctuations of the stock market. Unfavorable news immediately depresses prices, while favorable news raises them. The intrinsic values of stocks are not changed, but there is an immediate change in the thinking of the market operators, which is reflected at once in the minds of the holders. Not what will actually happen, but what security holders *believe* will happen causes them to buy or sell.

In the Depression years—and there may be years like them in the future—we saw this same suggestive force working overtime. Day after day we heard expressions such as, "Times are hard," "Business is poor," "The banks are failing," "Prosperity hasn't a chance," and wild stories about business failures on every hand, until they became the national chant. Millions believed that prosperous days would never return. Hundreds, yes thousands, of strong-willed men go down under the constant hammering, the continuous tap-tapping of the same fearful thoughts. Money, always sensitive, runs to cover when fear suggestions begin to circulate, and business failures and unemployment quickly follow. We hear thousands of stories of bank failures, huge concerns going to the wall, etc., and people readily believe them and act accordingly.

There will never be another business depression if people generally realize that their own fearful thoughts literally create hard times. They think hard times, and hard times follow. So it is with wars. When peoples of the world stop thinking of depressions and wars, they will become non-existent, for nothing comes into our economic sphere unless we first create it with our emotional thinking.

Dr. Walter Dill Scott, eminent psychologist and long president of Northwestern University, told the whole story when he said, "Success or failure in business is caused more by mental attitudes even than by mental capacities."

You may have read of the night of October 20, 1938, when Orson Welles and his Mercury Theater players broadcast a dramatization of H. G. Wells' novel, *The War of the Worlds*. It was a story of an invasion by some strange warriors from the planet Mars, but it caused fright among thousands of people. Some rushed out-of-doors, police stations were beseiged, eastern telephone exchanges were blocked, New Jersey highways were clogged. In fact, for a few hours following the broadcast, there was genuine panic among millions of listeners who believed our earth was being attacked by invaders from Mars. Yes, indeed, belief does cause some strange and unusual happenings!

Human beings are human beings the world over, all subject to the same emotions, the same influences, and the same vibrations. And what is a big business, a village, a city, a nation but merely a collection of individual humans controlling and operating it with their thinking and believing? As individuals think and believe, so they are. As a whole city of them thinks, so it is; and as a nation of them think, so it is. This is an inescapable conclusion. Every person is the creation of himself, the image of his own thinking and believing. As King Solomon put it, "For as he thinketh in his heart, so *is* he."

Rallies held in schools and colleges just before important athletic contests are based on the same principles—speeches, songs, and yells become the means of creating suggestion and arousing the will to win. Many sales managers employ the same principle in their morning sales meetings when frequently music is used to emotionalize the salesmen and to get the idea over to them that they *can* beat all their previous sales records. The same principle with varying technique is basic in the Army—in fact, all armies. The commands and formations constantly repeated in close-order drill develop in the men instant obedience, which ultimately becomes instinctive. The commands and formations become so fixed in their minds and bodies that their movements are almost automatic—all of which in turn creates that self-confidence which is absolutely necessary in active conflict.

It is very important to remember that the subconscious will go into action at once under the impetus of the commands or suggestions it receives from the conscious mind (or which come from outside sources and are transmitted to it via the conscious mind). But it gets results quicker if the conscious mind accompanies its message with a mental picture of the desired goal. It may be faint, sketchy, or even unfinished, but even if only an outline, it will be enough for the subconscious to act upon.

And this brings us to the rituals and ceremonies performed amid dramatic settings in churches and secret orders, all designed to appeal to the emotions and to create a mystical picture in the beholders' minds. These rituals, no matter what the setting, are there to hold your attention and link these symbols' hidden meanings with the particular ideas to be implanted in your mind. Various lighting arrangements, different paraphernalia, often a special garb for those directing the operations, all to the accompaniment of soft, often religious, music, all help to put you in the proper emotional (and incidentally, receptive) state. The idea is as old as history. Not only the most civilized peoples but also the most primitive tribes have their characteristic ceremonials. Similar methods for impressing the individual are employed at mediumistic séances and crystal-gazing performances; even the gypsy phrenologist considers it a part of her "props." Without this atmosphere, which tends to make our conscious mind drowsy and even puts it temporarily to sleep, we would not be so easily convinced, for by itself, the desire to satisfy completely our longings for the mystical and miraculous is often not strong enough to permit conviction.

This is not said with any idea of being sacrilegious, but to present a picture of the historic method of appealing to the masses. Appeal by drama is the first step in arousing people's emotions, no matter for what purpose. Awakening and stirring their emotional interest prepares the way to approach their reasoning minds.

Could Aimee Semple McPherson, she with the long flowing white robe and picturesque auburn hair-do, have put over her great act of saving souls as well as achieving healings, without her superb understanding of the power of the dramatic? It's something to wonder about, because Billy Sunday in his best table-sliding act was a novice compared to Aimee when it came to showmanship and plain impressiveness. She with her many artifices and stage settings put on a most solemn performance, and her followers—on the Pacific Coast at least—declare that the results she got were real and lasting. This is no reflection on Mrs. McPherson, for her followers were very sincere and believed in her work, her teachings, and the results—and that's all that matters.

However, men and women with strong personal magnetism and great orators can get the same emotional effect without props or stage settings to aid them. They are masters of tone effects, emotional appeal, gesticulations, bodily movements, eye magnetism, etc., by which your attention is held and you yourself are thrown wide open to their driving appeal.

Let's consider charms, talismans, amulets, good-luck pieces, four-leaf clovers, old horseshoes, rabbits' feet, and countless other trinkets which thousands of people believe in. By themselves, they are harmless inaminate objects with no power. But when people breathe life into them by their thinking, they do have power, even though the power isn't in them *per se*. The power comes only with the believing—which alone makes them effective.

An outstanding illustration of this is found in the story of Alexander the Great and Napoleon. In Alexander's day, an oracle proclaimed that whoever unloosened the Gordian knot would become ruler of all Asia. Alexander cut the knot with one stroke of his sword—and rose to tremendous heights and power. Napoleon was given a star sapphire when a child, with the prophecy that it would bring him luck and some day make him Emperor. Could anything but the supreme belief in the prophecy have carried this great man to become Emperor of France? He and Alexander became supermen because they had supernormal beliefs.

A cracked or broken mirror isn't going to bring you bad luck unless you believe in it. But as long as the belief is fertilized, nurtured, and made a part of your inner self, believe it or not, it *is* going to bring you bad luck—because the subconscious mind always brings to reality what it is led to believe.

Bird and Tompkins' *The Secret Life of Plants* claimed there are people with certain mind powers which, when directed at plant life such as grain, vegetables, flowers, and trees, can make them grow more abundantly. A number of years ago we had an old Swiss gardener who insisted that we replace a number of small trees and shrubs in our yard. At first I couldn't see the reason for digging up the old ones and replanting others, but the old man's insistence prevailed. I observed that while planting them, just after he got the small trees in the soil and covered the roots, he engaged in some sort of audible Mumbo Jumbo. He did the same with the shrubs. One day, my curiosity piqued, I asked him what he was mumbling about as he placed the trees and shrubs in the ground. He looked at me searchingly for a moment, then said, "You may not understand, but I'm talking to them, telling them they must live and bloom. It's something I learned as a boy from my teacher in the old country. Anything that grows should have encouragement, and I'm giving it to them." Certain humans appear to have a kind of affinity for plants, which the plants seem to feel. Thousands of professional gardeners will plant seeds only at certain times of the moon. Superstition, you say? Perhaps it is practical mysticism. The Yale investigators concluded that electrical fields play a major part in plant life, and certainly that is a scientific observation.

It is a long way from Switzerland to British Columbia, but in that Canadian province is a tribe of Indians, the members of which always talk to their lines and hooks before actually starting to fish, claiming that if they didn't, the halibut and salmon wouldn't bite. Many are the tales of South Sea Islanders who offer food to their tools and implements, talking to them as though they were alive and beseeching them to get results. It isn't a great jump from those customs to the blessings offered at ship launchings or at sailing times of large fishing fleets in civilized countries, where prayers are offered even today, for successful voyages or ventures.

I recall a thrifty neighbor of mine who, although a man of intelligence and mature years, had his hair cut at only certain times of the moon. I don't remember whether it was when the moon was waxing or waning, but he maintained that whatever phase he selected caused his hair to grow less abundantly than if he had visited the barber at other times. I asked him once where he got such an idea. He glared at me as though I were belittling his intelligence, and I never did get an answer to my question.

What I have said about plant and animal life may cause a lot of materialistic people to take violent issue, but it must be remembered that at work in the world are many forces of which we know little or nothing. Consider how many new principles were developed in World War II. In the late 1940s, the American Rocket Society made application to the United States Government for land on the moon. Perhaps the application was made in a spirit of facetiousness, but Americans landed on the moon only 20 years later.

Without question, human imagination, visualization, and concentration are the chief factors in developing the subconscious mind's magnetic forces. You have often heard the statement, "Hold that pose!" That, of course, means holding the mental picture or vision. Here again, suggestion—repeated suggestion—plays its part.

For example, you would like a new home. Your imagination goes to work. At first, you have only a hazy idea of the kind of house you would like. Then, as you discuss it with other members of your family—or ask questions of builders or look at illustrations of new houses—the mental picture becomes clearer and clearer, until you can visualize your ideal house in *all* its particulars.

After that, the subconscious goes to work to provide you with that house. It may come into manifestation in any number of ways. But do you really care whether you build it with your own hands, or whether it comes to you through purchase, or from the actions of outsiders? How it comes to you is of no great consequence!

When you are after a better job or planning a vacation trip, the process is the same. You've got to see it in your mind's eye, see yourself as holding that job or actually taking the trip. Some of our fears become realities through our imaginations, just as Job's did. Fortunately, many of them do not—as long as we hold the mental picture only temporarily, or at least not long enough to focus it fully upon the screen of our subconscious. The Biblical warning, "Where there is no vision, the people perish," is a fundamental truth, whether considered individually or collectively. For without the mental picture of accomplishment, little is done. You want a better job? You'll get it when you give your subconscious mind a mental picture of yourself holding that job.

As I write this, I think of the many experiences confided to me by those who have used this science during the years. I want to give you some of their stories, for in them you may perhaps find clues to an even more effective use of the principles and the mechanics which I am setting forth.

A friend got the idea of building a boat. He knew nothing about boat construction, but believed that with some simple instructions, he could build one. So he went ahead. In the course of the work, he found that he needed an elecrtric drill, but he didn't want to spend $75 or $80 for the kind he wanted, especially when he would be using it for only a few months. First, he tried renting a drill, but inasmuch as he could use it only at night and had to return it early the next morning, he found such an arrangement very inconvenient.

He told me, "I got to thinking one night that somewhere there was a drill for me and I would have it placed in my hands. The more I thought about it, the more I thought it possible. However, nothing happened for several days; then one evening a friend who owned a sizable garage—a man I hadn't seen for a couple of years—came to see me. He, too, was interested in boats, and hearing that I was building one, said he'd like to look it over. He saw me floundering around with the heavy half-inch drill I was using and asked me where I got it. I told him I had rented it and he laughed, saying, 'Come over to the shop tomorrow and I'll lend you a smaller one which you can handle much easier.' Needless to say, I got it and kept it during all the period I was constructing the boat.

"A somewhat similar experience happened when I was cutting the ribs. I found that a small jig saw wouldn't cut through three-quarter-inch lumber. Then I caught myself wishing for a band saw—that thought led me to a woodworking shop a few blocks away from my house. I could use the band saw if I paid the owner fifty cents an hour for its use. However, I found that I was running to and from my home, first to fit the ribs and then to shape them, and losing much time in the process. I frequently said to myself during those days that there must be some easier way to get the use of a band saw, and there was.

"The following Sunday another friend came to see how the boat was getting along. When I told him that I had been slowed down without the use of a band saw, he too laughed, saying, 'I bought one Thursday and won't be using it for some time. Got to get my shop fixed up, and in the meantime, you're welcome to use it.' As a matter of fact, he delivered it to me that same day and I kept it a number of months. I finished the boat!"

Another man told me how he got the use of a thirty-foot extension ladder with which to paint his house. "I thought I would undertake the painting in my spare time," he told me, "and began looking around to find where I could get the use of a ladder. I found places where I could rent one, but their fixed time requirements didn't fit into my plans. I don't know how many times I said to myself, You're going to find a ladder. And I did. It was Memorial Day, and while in my back yard, I happened to notice that a neighbor across the street was using a long ladder to wash off the walls of his house. I called to him, asking where he got the ladder. He told me he had bought it when he purchased the house. That afternoon it was in my back yard, and I had the loan of it for several weeks!"

Another man told me that shortly after Pearl Harbor, he had been looking for a garbage can of a certain size, but because of wartime priorities, he was unable to locate what he wanted. He visited second-hand stores, junk shops, bakeries, and garages to find the kind of container he wanted, but without success. He was about to give up hope when one morning he noticed workmen making repairs on a concrete building across from his home. They were using some waterproofing material from exactly the kind of can he had pictured for his own use. He asked the man in charge of the work what would be done with the container when the work was finished, and was told it would be left on the ground to be hauled away. He then explained his wants, and a couple of days later the container was in his garage—the workmen had not only emptied it but had washed and scrubbed it before delivery!

I had taken my car to a shop owner for repairs to the ignition system, after several mechanics had failed to locate the trouble. I told him how the car had been acting, and after listening he said, "I believe I can fix it."

I casually remarked, "Belief is a great thing, isn't it?"

"You bet it is. Thought is the greatest force in the world, and the dumb ducks laugh when you talk about it," he answered rather caustically.

"I don't, I'm interested," I replied. "Tell me of some instances where you have demonstrated the power of thought."

"I could keep you here all day telling you of its power—at least in my own life."

"Tell me a few. When did you first become aware of it?"

"Oh, I guess about twelve years ago, when I fell and broke my back. I was in a cast for a long time, and the doctors told me that even if I recovered, I would be crippled the rest of my life. As I lay on my back in the hospital worrying about my future, I frequently thought of the words used by my mother to the effect that 'One just has to believe.' One day it dawned on me that if I could hold on to the mental picture I was going to be all right, and if I believed in it sufficiently, I could get well. To make a long story short, here I am crawling over and underneath cars, and far from being a cripple, as you can see for yourself."

"Very interesting," I urged. "Tell me more."

"Well, I've used it frequently to get more business. As a matter of fact, this present location is a result of it. As you know, I was burned out at my old place a few weeks ago and space like this in the city is well-nigh impossible to find. For two or three days, I worried about not being able to find another location and deliberated whether I should attempt to go to work for someone else. Then one night I made up my mind I would continue in business for myself. That was the turning point. Just before I went to sleep I said to myself, 'Oh, you'll find a place within the next few days. This thought power hasn't failed you yet.' I went to sleep with full confidence that the place would be forthcoming. The very next day I went over to see the painter where I had taken the car I saved from the fire and mentioned I was looking for another place. 'That's funny,' he commented, 'You can rent this space. I've just bought the building in the next block from an owner who wanted to retire.' And so now here I am, on a main thoroughfare and with more business than I can possibly handle!"

I know that some readers will say that these are merely coincidences, but my files are filled with similar "coincidences." To some of you they may be just that, but those acquainted with this science know that these things come about as the result of intensified thought or mental picture-making. However, we come again to a matter of opinion—the difference in conclusions between those who think this is all nonsense and those who know that the things we think materialize after their kind. Again we are reminded of what Paracelsus said: "Men devoid of the power of spiritual perception are unable to recognize anything that cannot be seen externally."

It is pretty well agreed that the subconscious mind works as a result of images thrown upon its screen, but if there is something wrong with your projection apparatus or the original slide, then the projected image is blurred, inverted, or a total blank. Doubts, fears, counterthoughts, all manage to blur the pictures you consciously desire to project.

Those who have well-developed imaginations, such as great artists, writers, and inventors, possess the ability to visualize or to make mental pictures almost at will. However, with the mechanics which I will enlarge upon later and the explanations already given, anyone following them should have no difficulty in being able to see in his mind's eye the things, objects, or situations that he desires in reality.

One of the greatest fishermen I ever knew used this visualizing method. He could sit in a boat with one or two others and pull trout after trout out of the water, while his companions—using the same kind of bait and with apparently the same mechanical technique— dropped their hooks in the same places repeatedly, without results.

I asked him about it one time, and he laughingly replied: "I put the old 'squeeza-ma-jintum' [his word for magic] on them. I figuratively or mentally get down there where they are, and tell them to hook the bait or fly. In other words, I see them snapping at the hook and believe that it will work. That's all I can give you in the way of explanation."

This story was told to another fisherman not blessed with the first fisherman's luck, and he scoffed at it. "Ridiculous," he declared. "Any good fisherman must know the stream, the holes, the habits of fish, the type of bait or flies to use, and he'll catch them if they are there." However, he couldn't explain how others skilled in fishing technique could fish in an identical spot and still not catch them like the man who used the old "squeeza-ma-jintum."

Ben Hur Lampman was associate editor of *The Oregonian*, author of many articles and books on fishing and kindred subjects and a recognized naturalist. Upon reading this story, he said:

> *The man who says that it is ridiculous to consider there's some sort of magic or attraction at work makes himself ridiculous by displaying his ignorance. I can't explain how your friend is always so fortunate in making his catches beyond saying that there is decidedly something psychic about successful fishing. Anyone who has studied the habits of fish and tried to catch them, sooner or later realizes that there is more to successful fishing than merely throwing a lure or bait into a place where the fish are supposed to be. Just what the relationship is between mind and fish—if any—I cannot explain. But having been a student of fish, their ways and habits practically all my life, I do know that in successful fishing there is an unexplainable element or factor at work—call it what you please. Undoubtedly in the realm of psychic phenomena lies the explanation of the so-called fisherman's "luck" or the "squeeza-ma-jintum" of your successful fisherman friend.*

I am not a fisherman, but surely if this law of attraction works in other ways, there is no reason why it could not be used advantageously in fishing.

For many years I was interested in the game of golf and was a member of several clubs. I frequently played with a man who had been one of the world's tennis champions in his younger days. He was one of the most amazing short-shot players on the Pacific Coast. With his mashie or mashie niblick, he could place the ball on any desired spot on the green with a dead stop, as close to or as far from the pin as he desired, and he was usually down in one putt. His putting, too, was an art to marvel at.

One day he amazed everyone is our foursome with what could be called phenomenal shots. "How did you do it, George?" I asked.

"Well," he replied, "you've played handball and squash, and you know what it means to place your shots on the front wall. You intuitively place it high or low or so it will rebound to a side wall or result in a kill or an extremely low ball. I learned placement years ago in tennis. You have sort of a mental picture where you want the ball to go or land before you hit it with your racquet. I use the same principle with my short shots and putting. In other words, when I face the green and before I swing my club, I have an instant mental picture of where I want the ball to land, and when I putt, I actually see the ball dropping into the hole. Of course, a proper stance and knowledge of handling the clubs are vital. But most golfers have that and still don't get results. It is true that I spend many hours in practice. So do others; but the main thing is that I just seem to know where the ball is going to land before the club hits it. There's a confidence or a belief existing that I can do it, and with a mashie or mashie niblick I cause a backspin that will bring the ball to a dead stop when it lands."

For you who may raise your eyebrows at this, let's examine the facts given in a newspaper story written in the middle thirties by the famous sports writer, Grantland Rice. Rice declared that the phenomenal amateur golf player, John Montagu, could run rings around anyone. The ball always landed where he wanted to place it, whether 300 yards down the fairway or a chip shot to within two or three feet of the cup, and then when he putted, it was like the crack of doom. Rice said that the ball went where Montagu wanted it to go. Now let's read Montagu's own explanation as given in the same newspaper story. "Golf to me is played with the head, mind or brain or whatever you wish to call it. Of course, there are fundamentals of stance, grip, swing; but I must have a clear, clean mental picture of what I am doing before I play the shot. That mental picture takes charge of the muscular reaction. If there is no mental picture—what happens is a mere guess. This means almost endless concentration of thought if you are under pressure, and there is no thrill in any game unless you are under pressure."

Gene Sarazen, one of the greatest golf professionals of all times, used similar methods in his matches. His little book, *Golf Tips*, has much to say about mental pictures, objectives, concentration, and confidence. All golfers have heard of "mental hazards." In reality, they are bunkers, traps, water hazards, etc. But in the imaginations of many, they are formidable handicaps that put fear into the hearts of the players.

On one course where I often played there was a water hole. The distance from the tee to the hole was about one hundred and twenty yards spanning a small pond approximately fifty feet wide—an easy shot with a mashie or a mashie niblick for the average player. For a long time one member of the club, who had been a great baseball and football player in his younger days, could never get over this water hazard. Invariably he would put ball after ball into the water with his irons, to the accompaniment of profanity on his part and laughter on ours. Finally, as the months went by he took to using his spoon and hitting the ball far beyond the green.

One day I said to him, "I know the water fools you, but the next time, just blot out of your mind the picture of water between the tee and the green and see instead, mentally, an easy short fairway before you." The first time he followed the suggestion, his ball fell a few inches from the pin. And from that time, on, he later told me, as long as he followed the blotting-out technique, he never had any trouble. But when he was unable to concentrate on his own mental picture, due to the joshing from other members of his foursome, he landed in difficulties.

In observing many pool and billiard games, I am convinced that certain skilled players influence the direction and fall of the balls by mind control, although they may be in complete ignorance of the power they are using. If it can work on a golf ball, it certainly can work on a billiard ball.

The naturalist Roy Chapman Andrews told the story of a man from San Antonio, Texas, who with a .22 calibre rifle fired more than 14,500 shots at small blocks of wood tossed into the air without a single miss. Mr. Andrews emphasized his perfect timing and remarkable accuracy. Nothing was said of the mind-pictures; but if you have ever done any prolonged trap or target shooting, you know the part visualizing plays.

One finds the same sort of "magic" at work in all fields of sports. Great baseball batters, expert forward-passers in football, accurate drop-kickers—all consciously or unconsciously picture connecting with the ball and placing it where they want it to go. Certainly, practice and timing all have their primary importance, but the mental side must never be overlooked.

In this connection, I was impressed by several statements made by Dr. Marcus Bach in one of his first books, *They Have Found a Faith*. Dr. Bach tells of bowling with Father Divine, and of observing—from the way Father Divine selected a ball, and from his stance and delivery—that he was no bowler. Yet Father Divine made a strike on his first try and it was one of the prettiest strikes Dr. Bach ever saw. "Father's nonchalance was characteristic. He rubbed the soft palms of his hands together as if to say, 'Well, what do you expect when the Lord rolls one!'"

Dr. Bach also wrote of an interview with Rickert Fillmore, manager of Unity City and son of one of the founders of the Unity movement. Dr. Bach asked if the works of Unity could be applied to a real estate venture. Mr. Fillmore replied, "If it works at all, it works everywhere."

Many readers of this book may not be golfers or billiard players, but a simple experiment will demonstrate to you this strange power of attraction through visualizing—or making the mental picture actually work. Find a few small stones or pebbles which you can easily throw and locate a tree or post between 6 and 10 inches in diameter. Stand away from it twenty-five or thirty feet and start throwing the pebbles in an attempt to hit it. If you have average aim, most of the stones will go wide of their mark. Now stop and tell yourself that you can hit the objective. Get a mental picture of the tree figuratively stepping forward to meet the stone or of the pebble actually colliding with the tree in the spot where you want it to strike, and you'll soon find yourself making a perfect score. Don't say it's impossible. Try it, and you'll prove it can be done—if only you will believe it.

In the early days of wartime gasoline rationing, most people didn't consider getting additional coupons a criminal offense. A friend found he didn't have enough gas to take him to his duck lake. One Sunday he told me how he had secured enough coupons to make several trips to the shooting grounds. "I had just about given up the idea of duck shooting this fall when the thought occurred to me that I could put this Mind Stuff to work and get some more gas. Of course, everyone around the office knew that I wanted to go duck shooting and most of them knew of my problem. Whether they passed out word to their friends I do not know, but I got more coupons than you could shake a stick at. I had a constant picture of going hunting and using my automobile and of someone giving me gasoline coupons. It may be hooey, but I got the coupons. Even a farmer friend gave me gas out of his allotment."

Now let's take this same science into the kitchen. Did it ever occur to you that the so-called good cooks use this same science, some consciously and others unconsciously? Two people can attempt to make the same kind of pie, use identical ingredients and follow instructions to the letter. One will be a failure while the other will be the last word in culinary achievement.

Why? In the first case, the one cook approaches pie-making with trepidation. She knows she has had pie failures in the past and worries how this one is going to come out. She doesn't have a perfect mental picture of an appetite-satisfying golden brown crust with a wonderful zestful filling. She's upset and nervous, and without her knowing it, her uneasiness is communicated to her pie-making. The second one is aware, she knows that her pie is going to be tops—and it is. That primary mental picture—her belief—makes it so.

If you are a mediocre chef but you like to cook—that's a very necessary requisite too—sell yourself on the idea that you can prepare superior dishes. You can do it, for you have the forces inside of you, and they will come to your aid if only you will believe in them and call upon them. So put your heart and soul into the next pie you make. Envision it as perfect, and you will be surprised when you see the realization of your mental picture.

The same law will work no matter where it is applied, and that goes for everything from fishing to money-making or success in business. Let's take an example out of the war. When he left the

Philippines, General Douglas MacArthur declared "I shall return." With our Pacific Fleet in ruins at Pearl Harbor and with the Japanese in control of most of the South Pacific, MacArthur had no physical evidence that he would ever return. However, it was a statement of confidence or belief. He must have had a mental picture of his returning, and history relates how he kept his promise. Thousands of similar cases happened during the war and are happening today.

The art of
mental pictures

Once when I was in the investment banking business, Bob, a young salesman, came into my office for advice.

"I wish you would tell me how I can overcome my fear of Mr. Smith. I know I can sell him if I can just get in to see him and talk with him on his own level. As it stands, he's got the life scared out of me and every other salesman."

Mr. Smith, as I'll call him here, is a millionaire with a very imposing office organization. He is a portly type, with a heavy shock of hair and beetle-browed. Because of his growling manner, he easily scares timid folks. However, I knew he liked people who talked up to him.

I was momentarily puzzled, but the answer soon came. Bob had been picturing this man as he saw him. "You know he's not going to hurt you physically," I said. "Suppose you saw Mr. Smith at the beach in a bathing suit. You wouldn't be afraid of him there, would you, even though he did appear to be a pretty hairy fellow?"

"Certainly not," he replied. Then the idea of a hairy body came to me, and I asked, "Bob, did you ever see one of those clownish dancing bears wearing a fez or a dunce cap? You know they can growl, but most of them are toothless and can't bite."

"Sure," responded the salesman.

"Well, you have a good imagination. Just picture our friend as one of those harmless old bears, fez, collar, and all, and the mental hazard is gone, isn't it?"

Laughing heartily, Bob went out. A few days later he sold the man $20,000 worth of securities, and this executive may still be wondering how the young salesman ever got in to see him, to say nothing of selling him.

A couple of weeks later, Bob was back in my office, telling me how he had used similar methods in making another sale, this time to a gruff old man who wore white whiskers, had a patriarchal and stern appearance, and used a vitriolic tongue that was feared by most salesmen.

"That old goat had me buffaloed for a long time. I knew he had money, but every time I passed his store and saw him scowling—he was always scowling—I couldn't get up courage to go in and tackle him. A few days ago I got to thinking of the picture-making plan you told me to use on Mr. Smith and the idea popped into my head of a picture of Santa Claus. I said to myself, 'Sure, the old goat could be Santa Claus, and who's afraid of that kindly old boy?' Well, it worked there too. The old man was swell to me—sort of flattered that a young fellow like me dared approach him. I got a $5,000 order out of him and he told me to come back next week because he wanted to go over his whole security list with me. That means more business."

Many men holding executive positions assume an air of importance that causes some people to hold them in awe. With their elaborate office surroundings and their numerous secretaries and clerks, they put on a show that proves impressive to some. Just bear in mind that these executives are mere human beings with the same fears, frailties, and faults that are common to millions; at home they are often docile little souls. When you picture them as they really are, rather than as they appear or pretend to be, the mental hazard immediately disappears. The *genuinely* great man is usually easy to approach and seldom barricades himself from callers. If you are a salesman, this should give you a clue to how to eliminate the mental hazards that crop up when you visit someone who puts on a show of being superior.

A lawyer told me of an experience that nicely illustrates my point: "I once found myself pitted against an attorney who had a great reputation and was generally feared by younger men. For a little while in the courtroom, I admit I was frightened, but I closed my eyes and said to myself, 'I'm just as good as he is; as a matter of fact, I'm better. I can lick him and I will.' I repeated words and phrases like that for several seconds, and when I opened my eyes, I could have licked two like him. I now go through the same little ritual whenever I get a tough case or the jury doesn't look favorable. Maybe it's luck, maybe it's all illusory, but it always works."

People who act and appear hard-boiled are usually softies at heart and once an interviewer eliminates the mental hazard, he has licked the situation. Take a couple of deep breaths the next time you call on one, convince yourself he'll be a push-over, and he will.

During the Depression of the 'thirties, a group of managers and assistant managers, including the butchers of a large grocery chain store, came on their own initiative to me for help. After a six weeks' course, the men decided to put the lectures into effect. It was agreed that each store one day a week would use the science I had expounded to push the sale of certain items. After considerable debate, among the items selected for the test were cheese, rolled roasts, salmon, and just plain Hubbard squash, since the manager of a store in one of the outlying districts had said he could make a good buy of squash from a farmer. The day before each sale, the managers carefully coached their clerks to make a mental picture of each customer coming into their stores and buying the selected items. Of course, prominent displays were made of each item, and each clerk was instructed to think of selling the special item whenever a customer appeared.

The results were astounding. The store specializing in cheese sold more cheese in that one day than had passed over the counter in a six months' period; the shop which specialized in the rolled roasts on Saturday had them sold before noon; the store which had featured fresh salmon on Friday sold more salmon than all the other stores of the group combined. The one where squash had been selected had to call upon the farmer twice during the day to replenish the supply.

Fifteen years later, with only one exception (and he was a war casualty), each man who took the lecture course was either in business for himself or had a much better job. As a matter of fact, one of the men came to own three stores of his own, while another became manager of a chain of stores in a neighboring state.

I think of a recent conversation with the head of a large Pacific Coast advertising agency, who for a number of years handled the sales promotion work for a well-known coffee manufacturer who had recently sold his business.

"If there was ever a man who used this stuff to tremendous advantage," declared the advertising executive, "it was that old man. He came to this section as a kid and learned the coffee roasting and blending business. He concluded that he could do better if he were in business for himself. He thoroughly believed that he could blend the best coffee, and even up to the time of his retirement, after years in the business, he thoroughly believed that his coffee was the best on the market. Of course, that belief made the old man a millionaire."

I once gave a printer a small manuscript that dealt with the subject we are now considering; I wanted to get it out in pamphlet form. The next morning he popped into my office, almost out of breath and visibly shaking. Naturally I asked if there were anything wrong. "Just had the oddest experience," he spluttered. "I took your manuscript home last night and read it, and I said to myself, 'If the stuff actually works as the author claims, then I ought to be able to find a parking space close to his office when I go to see him.' I thought no more about it until I was driving from our plant to your office just a few minutes ago, and then the thought again occurred to me that it might work. Well, I turned the corner, and there wasn't a space to be seen on Sixth Avenue, and I was going to dismiss it all as bunk. But as I slowed down to let some pedestrians pass, I saw a car pull away from the curb right in front of this building and there was my place. It gives me goose-pimples. Maybe it's just one of those things."

"Perhaps," I said, "but why not try it again?"

He did, and had similar results over a period of years. Call them coincidences if you like. But this printer never would—especially when shortly afterward he was able to more than triple his business while most printers were having a difficult time getting any orders at all.

Now and then I told acquaintances about the printer's experiences and was astounded to learn that others seemed able to find parking space as had this printer. One woman, a Unity student, told me that she and her sister never drove downtown without saying that they would find a parking space in or near a spot that they desired—and they always found one.

A woman, a dietician and instructor in a large hospital, said to me, "The working of this power, or whatever it is, often frightens me. As an illustration, this happens with continued frequency. Every morning on my way to work when I enter the business section, the traffic lights always turn green and I get through all of them without a stop. I cannot recall the time that the lights have shown red against me. Now I just take it all as a matter of course."

A few months ago a woman was arrested for violating the traffic signals, but according to the newspaper stories at the time, she convinced the judge that the green light was on when she crossed the intersection. She was a motherly woman, and the judge freed her when she told him, "Judge, the light just had to be green, and it always is for me because I keep repeating as I near an intersection 'Green light be on, green light be on.' "

The police maintained, however, that there were no signals at this intersection—only the flashing intermittent red light. But here was the motherly old lady convincing the judge of her belief! Obviously she believed in her ability to have the signals the way she wanted them.

A woman told me of driving cross-country from Washington, D.C., to join her husband who had been assigned to duty in a Pacific Coast city. "I was frightened in the beginning," she said. "I had never driven any such distance alone in my life. One day I got to thinking of my grandmother who had been one of the pioneers to the Pacific Northwest and who had done many things alone. My fear was gone at once. However, the garage man who looked over my car before I started told me not to go without getting new tires; he said the old ones would blow out any time. If I hadn't been so intent on making the trip and without delay, I might have listened to him;

but the thought again came to me that they *would* last until I got across the country—and last they did. While I do not use the car much now, the original tires are still there, though in pretty bad shape. But no blowouts ever occurred."

Another case that reinforces my contention involves an oil refining company and more than a million dollars of investors' money. In its early days, the company experienced great financial difficulties brought on by suits and marketing problems. It became necessary to reorganize the whole financial structure, with the stockholders taking new securities but forgoing interest for a number of years. The stockholders were told to make a mental picture of the oil turning into money and coming from every still and every spigot—in short, to visualize the company as a money-maker. Incidentally, this company was in a field dominated by strongly intrenched major companies. Nevertheless, not only did the company become a substantial money-maker, but it was subsequently sold, and all the security holders got back their money with interest in full.

Jimmy Gribbo, once well-known to sports fans as a manager of prizefighters, made winners out of many boxers by teaching them how to visualize themselves as winners—and they became winners.

I realize that some readers, especially those who know nothing about Mind Stuff, will question these stories. But those who related them are of undoubted veracity, and I believe that many of my readers could relate much stranger tales from their own experiences.

G. N. M. Tyrrell, the well-known English investigator and writer, declared that if, while dwelling upon the activity of the subconscious mind, we determine upon an intention to do a certain thing, we may subconsciously initiate a train of events likely to bring this thing about. Dr. Shailer Mathews, long associated with the University of Chicago, stated "that we influence events by very great desires, and there is psychological proof on ourselves of the effects of our desires."

Here are two cases in point:

A woman who ran a large antique shop was a recognized authority whose advice concerning antiques was much sought after by other women. But she happened to dislike social activities and was constantly bothered by a woman who kept inviting her to luncheons and teas. This second woman merely wanted to be seen in the company of this renowned authority—who, however, kept declining her. Then a woman's club scheduled a well-known lecturer to talk, and under the second woman's insistent pleas, the head of the antique shop finally agreed to go with her.

"She caught me in an off moment," she told me, "and no sooner had I agreed than I began to regret having made the promise to go. The woman and I had nothing in common. As a matter of fact, she bored me. I hate those would-be highbrow affairs, and I was certain this was going to be one. At night I would actually have cold sweats thinking about what I had done and how I could get out of going without offending the woman—who was a fairly good customer of the store, and who, incidentally, I knew would have a lot of mean things to say about me should I fail to keep my agreement.

"I thought about it and thought about it, figuring on making up excuse after excuse—none of which seemed good enough or plausible. I was nearly beside myself. The day of the meeting was drawing near, and I had about decided to phone her, telling her that an important engagement had come up making it impossible to attend the lecture, when in she came.

"She was all apologies when she informed me that the lecture had been canceled. Did I draw a sigh of relief? I thoroughly believe in what you preach and I think that my thought had something to do with what happened. I know that some will say it was a coincidence—let them call it that if they please. But stranger things than that happen, and they're not all coincidences."

The second story involves the manager of a company manufacturing a hay fever remedy. He had recently arrived in town, found an apartment near his office, and sought a telephone for his apartment. At that time, just after the war, the telephone company had a long waiting list and was installing priority telephones only for doctors, police, fire officials, and those engaged in public emergency work.

For two months he tried to get a telephone, seeking out everyone he could to help him. Through a mutual friend, he learned that I knew the manager of the phone company and he came to see me. I quickly disillusioned him of the idea that I could persuade the manager to give him a telephone ahead of several thousand others, but I did tell him that he shouldn't have any trouble if he could establish his rights to a priority.

I asked him whom he had talked with, and he gave me the names of several people in major and minor positions with the company. Then he explained that it was imperative that he have a telephone, for he was the only one connected with his own company who could handle after-office-hour business.

"Do you have many long-distance calls?" I asked. "And how much does your company telephone business amount to a month?"

He gave me an unusually high figure for his monthly bills.

"Take your last few months' bills with you and see the man you saw first, look him straight in the eye and tell him that you've just got to have a telephone without delay," I told him, "but don't go near him until you can convince yourself that you can convince him. Otherwise, your task is futile. You've just got to make up your mind that you're going to have a telephone installed in your apartment, and you must believe it."

"I'll try it," he said, then quickly catching himself said, "No, I'll do it. I'll get that telephone."

He came to see me several days later.

"It certainly worked. I must tell you about this, for it's very funny how a positive thought brings about such a series of happenings. I went to see the man I had first talked with, and he was rather amazed that I had come back to him. This time I explained in detail why it was imperative that I have a phone and showed him the bills as you suggested. It was only a matter of minutes before I had him convinced. He was just about to call the manager to plead my cause when, lo and behold, the manager called him on some other matter. Then this man told my troubles to the manager who agreed I was entitled to a priority. He suggested that I see someone in charge of priority ratings.

"I had never heard of this man and before that time had known nothing of the priority system. I told this man my story and a lot about our business, referring to the antihistamines we manufactured. I nearly collapsed when he told me that he was bothered by hay fever and had tried various remedies without results. From then on, it was a natural. It all gives me a sort of spooky feeling. How did it happen that the manager called the man I was talking with at that particular time, and how did it happen that the man with the final say-so was a hay fever victim and one I could help? From now on, send me the scoffers."

Of course, we all know that our thoughts determine our carriage, our facial expression, our conversation, for what we are outwardly comes as the result of what we think habitually. Many women have improved their appearance by continuing to feel the delights of beauty, by thinking thoughts of the beautiful, by wearing stylish clothes, by adding things of beauty to their surroundings, by developing poise and easy carriage, and by constantly telling themselves that they are going to win out. You have seen in movie plays how a badly dressed, ordinary-looking girl can be transformed into a most attractive woman by beautiful clothes and the latest hair-do. You can do the same thing—and will speed up the process if you continue to hold the mental picture of your new self and never relax for a second.

Most people dread going to a dentist. It isn't so much what happens as what the patients *think* will happen that brings on the jitters. Again we have thoughts creating conditions that we would go a long way to avoid. The *American Weekly* of July 7, 1940 told of a children's dentist in Pittsburgh who fixed up a playroom adjoining his operating room and fitted it up with toys, sandboxes, blocks, etc. The idea was to get the children interested in playing and get their thoughts off the coming work on their teeth. Once in the chair, the children were encouraged to talk about anything but their teeth. The dentist even attached a button switch to his electric drill line that the children themselves could turn on and off, and assured them before he started work that they could turn off the current at the slightest indication of pain. His practice was enormous.

A barber who has built up a large clientele among small children has on his stands numerous well-illustrated, children's books, which he puts in his little patrons' hands as he places them in his chair. He gets them interested in the pictures before he starts cutting their hair. "Once in a while it doesn't work," he said, "especially if the child hasn't been taught to look at pictures. Then I have to bring out the mechanical toys, such as those that utter throaty sounds or squeaks when they are squeezed. But the trick is to get the kids to forget about their hair being cut. Once that is done, I have no trouble."

Imagination or mental picture-making can often produce queer results. Fear is basically an imaginary factor, as millions of men who went through the war will testify. You suddenly receive a telegram, and before you open the envelope, you fear you'll hear bad news—and you promptly get a sinking feeling in the pit of your stomach. The news may be good, but for the moment you are shaken with fear, and only the good news relieves you of that nervousness.

The story is often told of a man who got the only room left in a hotel. It was ordinarily a storage room, but when the hotel was crowded, it doubled as a bedroom. During the night, the man complained of lack of air. On arising, he groped through the dark to what he thought was the window. He couldn't open it, and, after finding a shoe, knocked out the pane of glass. Then he slept comfortably the rest of the night, only to discover at dawn that the window was still intact. What he had smashed was the glass door to a closet!

During World War II, Margaretta West related a somewhat similar story in *This Week*. Returning on a troopship from the South Pacific, she found herself packed into a cabin with seventeen other women. Because of the black-out rules, the portholes had been closed, and the cabin was stifling. Inasmuch as the ship was not sailing until morning, permission was granted to open the portholes after everyone was in bed. Miss West tells how she undertook to open the portholes and how everyone was pleased that they could then sleep. And sleep they all did. But on awakening in the morning, they found that Miss West had opened only the inner portholes. The outer ones remained closed, shutting out both light and air during the night.

During food rationing, thousands of people ate margarine in the home of friends, thinking it to be butter. During Prohibition days, it was a common practice to pour moonshine whiskey into bottles with apparently genuine labels, and many did not know the difference. Sometimes the lowly carp has been served as red snapper, without any gourmet being the wiser.

In countless ways science has proved the effects of the workings of the imagination. Postage stamps have been placed on the skin of patients who believed that they were small mustard plasters; blisters developed under the stamps. By ringing a bell when he offered food to dogs, the Russian scientist Pavlov soon had the animals associating the bell with the thought of food, and it was only a short time before the mere ringing of the bell caused their stomachs to secrete digestive juices. Sit at a restaurant counter and notice an enticing dish placed before your neighbor. At once you become hungry and your mouth begins to water.

The peeling of onions often causes tears to flow from the person doing the peeling. Yet the mere sight of an onion being peeled by another person several feet away—and with no odor permeating the air—can bring tears to the eyes of others in the room. Some people cannot eat warmed-up leftovers, declaring that they make them sick. Undoubtedly, some spoiled leftovers eaten years before did upset their stomachs, and the mental picture never left them. Others claim that they must take soda after every meal to help them digest their food—which medical authorities say is often merely the working of their imaginations. A sudden emotional shock under the pressure of your imagination will cause your skin to turn cold and may even be followed by alternate sweats and chills. When your imagination goes to work, something your physician has told you can have a terrifying effect.

I have crossed the Atlantic and Pacific Oceans several times and have never been seasick, even in the most severe storms and violent pitchings and rollings of the ship—except once; and that was when I had to help another passenger who was violently ill. However, early in my travelings I learned to look away from those who were seasick, realizing that a suggestive force could make me run for the rail.

Try sucking a lemon when a friend near you is whistling. The mere sight of it will stop him, and all because the thought of the sour lemon puckers up his mouth and makes whistling impossible.

While lecturing, in order to prove the power of the imagination, I would often hold up two small atomizers containing different colored fluids. I would tell my audience that one contained lilac perfume and the other attar of roses, explaining that my experiment would determine the difference in my listeners' perceptive powers. I would then turn my back on the audience so that they could not see which atomizer I was spraying into the air. At the same time, I called upon them to identify the odor. Some would say lilac, others attar of roses. Of course, there was always great chagrin when these two groups discovered that their imaginations had led them astray, and that both atomizers contained nothing but colored—odorless—water.

In his little essay, *Concerning Tobacco,* Mark Twain (who had the reputation of smoking the worst cigars) says that a man thinks he can tell what he regards as a good cigar from what he regards as a bad one—but he can't. He goes by the brand, yet imagines he goes by the flavor. Twain tells how he borrowed from a wealthy friend a double handful of forty-cent cigars bearing red-and-gold bands that signified their quality. Twain removed the bands and put the now unbranded cigars into his own box. He passed them out to friends at the end of a dinner. Believing them to be the cheap cigars that Twain smoked, his friends all tossed them away after two or three whiffs. Unquestionably, there is a difference in the taste of even domestic cigars and cigarettes, but the imagination plays an important part in determining it.

When you realize that inventors, artists, scientists, architects, and builders of great companies all must employ their imagination, you get some idea of its magnitude. Shakespeare said, "Assume a virtue if you have it not." Let's follow some of the implications of this great advice. In assuming a virtue, you are assuming it via your imagination. To become the person you would like to be, you must create a mental picture of your newly conceived self, and if you continue to hold it, the day will come when you are that person in reality. So it is with the accomplishment of desires.

But here we must make a distinction between daydreaming and a true mental picture—the proper use of the imagination. Perhaps some genie will drop $100,000 into your lap or provide you with a luxuriously furnished mansion overnight, but I have never had the pleasure of meeting one. Daydreaming or mere undirected wishful thinking doesn't have the power to release the latent forces within you that will bring you one hundred thousand dollars or a mansion.

When you employ your imagination properly, you see yourself doing a thing, and then you go ahead and do it. Doing the thing you have pictured to yourself brings it into actual existence. In this connection, think about the use of a magnifying glass. When properly focused, it will gather and concentrate the light from the sun to burn a hole in the paper upon which the rays are focused. It must be held steady before the heat builds up. So it is with your images or mental pictures.

Dr. Emile Coué, the French doctor who threw so much light on the power of suggestion, declared that imagination was a much stronger force than will-power. When the two are in conflict, he said, the imagination always wins. For example, let's say you are an inveterate smoker of good cigars and decide to break yourself of the habit. You grit your teeth, shove out your chin, and solemnly declare that you are going to use your will-power to quit for good. Then suddenly comes the idea of the taste of a good cigar, its aroma and soothing effects—your imagination goes to work and out the window goes your resolution to break the bad habits.

Charles Fourier, the early 19th-century French philosopher, declared that the world's future would grow out of the brain of man and be shaped, controlled, and directed by the desires and passions by which men are moved. His prophecy is coming true, yet man has barely begun shaping and controlling the world through his mind.

All of this brings us to the topic of desire and what you actually want in life. Comparatively few people have really great desires. Most are content to go along filling the tiny niches in which they find themselves. They accept their positions in life as something that fate has fixed for them, and very seldom do they make either a mental or physical effort to extract themselves from those positions. They never raise their sights or realize that it's just as easy to shoot at a bird on a limb thirty feet above the ground as it is to shoot at the ground the same distance away. Many engage in wishful thinking—which by itself is without effect simply because the power factor is missing.

But when you run across a person who is really going to town—and there are many—you realize that his or her desire projects the greater power behind it all. The way seems easy for those people, and to a great degree it is, because they are putting to use the powers of their subconscious minds—which in turn magnetize, co-ordinate, and then transmit to their conscious minds electrifying visions of what they most desire.

So be reminded: whatever you fix your thoughts upon or steadily focus your imagination upon, that is what you attract. This is no mere figure of speech, but a fact that anyone can prove to his or her own satisfaction. Whether the results come through magnetic, electrical, or some other energy is still undetermined. But while man hasn't been able to define thought-attraction, its manifestations can be seen on every hand. It is like the electrical field itself—we do not know exactly what electricity is, although we know how to generate it through various material kinds of energy-producing apparatus; we see electricity manifest every time we turn on a light or snap a switch.

However, it is very difficult for the average person to concentrate for any length of time, to say nothing of holding a mental picture for any great period. You will find that countless thoughts, ideas, fantasies will ebb and flow through your mind with astonishing rapidity. You are constantly being swayed by what you read, see, and hear, and as a result, the co-ordinating part of this creative force gathers all these scattered elements together in a confused mass, instead of making a clear and dynamic picture of your desire.

That brings us to a system of mechanics by which anyone can focus thoughts so that they will penetrate to the deepest depths of the subconscious mind.

I have been in the private offices of a great many industrial leaders, business men, and bankers. And long before I understood this science of belief, I was impressed with the pictures, photographs, slogans, and bits of statuary to be found in the inner sanctums of great firms. In the office of the head of a great utility concern hung photographs of the industry's early leaders. In another office were pictures of the great financiers of history. In some there were busts of Napoleon, in others, little shrines or good-sized statues of Buddha. I saw offices where there hung on the walls such slogans as "We do the impossible—any place, any time", "If it can be done, we can do it", "Do it now", "Be a self-starter—don't wait to be cranked." It is reported that the private office of F.W. Woolworth, who became known as the Napoleon of business, was a replica of Napoleon's study. Undoubtedly many of you have seen or heard of such displays. But has it ever occurred to you what their purpose was?

There can be only one answer: that they serve as a constant reminder—getting the picture across to the occupant of the room that he can succeed as did those before him. Every time he looks around the room, a motto or a slogan meets his gaze. He sees the eyes of Napoleon upon him when he sits at his desk; he feels a touch of the spiritual as he gazes at the little shrine. In other words, executives use a form of mechanics to excite their imaginations—pictures to inspire them, or a series of suggesting forces that reach their subconscious minds. In the offices of many doctors (including some who would scoff at the great power of suggestion) hang the photographs of great men of medicine or famous teachers in medical schools. I have often wondered if the doctors realized the underlying power of these portraits.

When you realize that the subconscious works accurately to externalize whatever suggestion is most greatly impressed upon it, you then understand the necessity for concentrating and for constantly repeating one single suggestion.

Like other great men, Thomas A. Edison obviously knew the value of the repeated suggestion and made use of it. As part of the ceremonies celebrating the hundredth anniversary of the inventor's birth, his desk, sealed at his death, was opened on February 8, 1947. Conspicuous among the articles found in it was a piece of paper which bore the legend, "When down in the mouth, remember Jonah. He came out all right." Edison must have thought well of that expression and perhaps reflected much upon it, or else he would not have kept it on his desk before him.

Often I have likened this matter of desire and suggestion to the planting of vegetable or flower seeds. Once the soil is prepared and the tiny seeds are placed in it, it is only a short time before they put forth roots and sprouts begin to appear. They are determined to emerge from the ground. When they start upward through the soil in search of sunshine and moisture, obstacles mean nothing to them. If they can't push aside stones or bits of wood, they'll extend themselves and grow around them. They succeed, blossom, and give forth fruit, vegetables, or flowers unless some greater force destroys them. While we are not aware of the details of nature's secrets, we observe the seed buried for a long time in the dark, gradually expanding and exerting itself until it becomes a thing of beauty or usefulness. Cultivate it, attend it, give it sunshine and water, and it grows into full life. Remember it always produces after its kind, be it single or hybrid.

So it is with the suggestions you impart to your subconscious mind. The results will be pure or complex, depending upon the original seed and the attention you give it. In other words, plant the right kind of thought—of a pure strain—and habitually feed it with strong affirmative thought always directed toward the same end, and it will grow into a mighty force, finding ways and means of overcoming all obstacles. Its roots will reach forth to find more terrain on which to grow and expand its foliage to gather more illumination.

It was desire that brought progress to the world. Without it, we all would still be living in the Stone Age. Everything we have in our modern world is the result of desire. Indeed, desire is the motivating force of life itself. You see it all around you—in the animal kindgom, in all forms of plant life, and in all acts and operations of human beings. Hunger promotes a desire for food, poverty a desire for riches, cold a desire for warmth, inconvenience a desire for ease and efficiency.

Desire is the generating power of all human action, and without it no one can get very far. The keener, the more urgent the desire, the sooner its consummation. It marks the difference between the uneducated ditchdigger and the person of accomplishment, between the clerk and the executive, between the failure and the success. So you must always start with desire. Keep in mind that by the magic of believing, you can obtain what you picture in your mind's eye. The mechanics are there only to help you focus your desire-picture sharply on the screen of your subconscious mind, and let you shut out all distracting thoughts, negative ideas, or any fear or doubt projections that might otherwise penetrate to your subconscious.

So let's get down to the mechanics!

Secure three or four index cards. (Ordinary business-size cards will do.) Go to your office, your home, your room, or any other place where you can have privacy. Sit down and ask yourself what one thing you desire above everything else. When the answer comes and you are certain that it is your uppermost desire, then at the top of one card write a word picture of it. One or two words may be sufficient—"a job," "a better job," "more money," or "home of my own."

Then on each card duplicate the word picture on the original. Carry one in your billfold or handbag, place another alongside your bed or fasten it to your bedstead. Prop another on your shaving mirror or dressing table, and still another on your desk. If you bear in mind successful executives' custom of keeping in their offices pictures, mottoes, slogans, busts, and statues, you will appreciate that in using the cards you are utilizing the same forces, only in much more concentrated form. The whole idea, as you may have guessed, is to make you see the mental picture at all hours of the day. Just before going to sleep at night and upon waking in the mornings, concentrate upon your thoughts with added force. But don't stop with merely those two periods of the twenty-four hours. The more often you visualize your desire by this method (or by one of your own devising), the speedier its materialization will be.

At the start, you may have no idea of how the results are to come. Yet you need not concern yourself. Just leave it to the sub-conscious mind, which has its own ways of making contacts and of opening doors and avenues that you may have never even guessed at. You will receive assistance from the most unexpected sources. Ideas useful in accomplishing your program will come at most unexpected times. You may be suddenly struck with the idea of calling a person you have not heard from for a long time, or writing someone you have never seen before. You may get the impulse to read the newspaper or listen to the radio. Whatever the idea is, follow it.

Many successful people get ideas during the night that are immediately transcribed to a pad so they will not be lost. For many years before I thoroughly understood this science, I was associated with an executive who, after reaching his desk in the morning, would begin pulling notes out of his pocket. In a few minutes things would begin to hum. These notes might contain comments on various advertising media, an outline of a sales campaign, new purchases, or a rearrangement of the sales organization; but all of them contributed to the success of his operations. Keep a pad and pencil on a stand near your bed, and if ideas come during the night, note them down so that you won't forget them in the morning.

I recall the time when I put this science to work in order to save the firm of which I was then vice-president. All of the employees sat around in a half-circle, and as I began my remarks, I asked each man to provide himself with paper and pencil. Most of them thought that I wanted them to take notes. But there was considerable surprise when I told them to write down what they most wanted in life. I explained that if they would do this, I would point out the way to obtain it.

Two or three of the younger men laughed, but the older men, realizing that I was deadly earnest, did as I suggested. To the younger men I said simply: "If you want to hold on to your jobs, you'll do as I ask. For if this stuff doesn't work, we'll all be out on the street." They complied. I told them to show no one what they had written.

After the meeting, one of the younger men came to me to apologize for having laughed.

"That's all right, Bob," I told him.

"But it sounded so silly at first," he explained. "Imagine me getting a new automobile by simply writing it down. But after you explained the science of it all, I guess it does make sense."

Several years later, this chap came to my home and said he wanted to show me something. There along the curb was parked his expensive new automobile.

In the years that followed, I found opportunities to ask those who attended that meeting if they had obtained what they had written down. Without exception, every man had. One had wanted a wife of a certain nationality. He got her, and there are two fine boys in the family. Another put down the figures of a very sizable fortune. He got it. Another man wanted a beach cottage, another a better home, and so on. Steadily through the years every one of these men has constantly made money, many of them averaging monthly more than they had ever made before in their lives, much to the astonishment of many others in the same line of business.

I cannot emphasize too strongly that you should tell no one

just what the words on the cards mean nor give anyone an inkling of what you desire. To do so may end disastrously for you. When you get a better understanding of this science, you can understand how thought vibrations—conscious or unconscious, because of envy or some other cause—can be set up to counteract your own.

To illustrate this, I am reminded of a doctor friend who applied for a commission in the Navy during the early days of World War II. He closed his office, told everyone that he was joining the Navy, and found himself the recipient of many parties and gifts. "It taught me a lesson never to tell anyone of my plans or desires," he laughingly told me later. "It was two years before I received notice of assignment, and meanwhile I had to go back into private practice. It certainly was embarrassing to get all those various farewell gifts, only to cool my heels at home for two years."

The truth is that when you talk about what you're going to do, you scatter your forces. You lose your close connection with the subconscious, and unless you do as directed here, you will frequently have to start all over again in your program of achievement.

"Go and tell no man" still holds true.

My readers will recall what I said before about Mumbo Jumbo, chants, incantations and affirmations. By engaging in them, you put the suggestive forces to work to stimulate your subconscious.

These repetitive words and phrases, said silently or aloud, are merely methods of convincing the subconscious mind—for auto-suggestion, no matter what the form, is the only way of molding its pattern. The subconscious is extremely receptive, and it can be convinced of whatever propositions you present to it. Be they true or false, positive or negative, once they are imbedded in the subconscious mind, it goes to work with all of its faculties and energies to materialize them in real life. The simpler the words to express the ideas you wish conveyed to the subconscious, the better. For example, if you are unhappy, use the words, "I am happy." You don't need the cards for this. Just repeat them to yourself twenty or thirty times. "I am strong," "I am happy," "I am convincing," "I am friendly," "Everything is fine" are a few simple affirmations you can use to change your mental point of view for the better. But if the effects are to be permanent, you must continue the affirmations until the desired results are obtained.

Through repetition, the person with a fixed goal, a clear picture of his desire, or ideal always before him causes it to be buried deeply in his subconscious mind and thus—thanks to its generative and sustaining power—realizes his goal in a minimum of time and with a minimum of physical effort. Just pursue the thought unceasingly. Step by step you will achieve realization, for all your faculties and powers become directed to that end.

Suppose you want a better job or a promotion. Not only use the cards, but keep telling yourself constantly and continuously that you are going to get that job. You have already visualized it if you have accepted this science, but the repetition will be the means of driving the suggestion deeply and firmly into your subconscious mind. This may be compared to driving a nail into a board. The first tap puts the nail in place, but only by a number of heavy blows is the nail driven home. Never forget that the subconscious mind will accept and carry out whatever it is powerfully instructed to do. A great example of power developed by repetition is the story of Milo and the calf. Every day he lifted the calf, until the day came when he was lifting a full-grown bull.

Think of all of this in terms of the so-called material things. You know that two objects cannot occupy the same space at the same time. Your mind can be compared to that space: you can't have very many negative thoughts or doubts if you keep your mind filled with positive, powerful, and creative thoughts. Consider your mind a room with a single door, and you have the only key. It rests with you to decide what is to come through the door—that is, whether you are dominated by positive or negative thoughts, and which ones you are going to admit—for your subconscious mind will respond to the vibrations of the thoughts that are strongest in you.

Alternately, compare your mind to a tank filled to the brim with clear, pure water. You cannot put any object into that tank without displacing some of the water and causing the tank to overflow. When you permit negative thoughts of doubt or fear to enter your consciousness, obviously some of your forceful, positive, creative thoughts will have to give way, and consequently you weaken your positive state. Thus, as long as you do not accept unfavorable vibrations, your subconscious mind will not be hindered by anything you may hear, see, or experience. In other words, you must keep your subconscious mind fed at all times with positive thoughts so that their strong vibrations will ward off all negative and destructive thoughts from the outside.

For years philosophers have taught that if we are to be happy, we must be busy working or doing something that holds our attention. Freud claimed that happiness arises from only two abilities—being able to work, and to love. The explanation is that when we concentrate on some pleasant task or individual, our minds are no longer open to roving and undesirable vibrations. That is why many doctors advise business and professional men to take up hobbies to divert their minds from thoughts of worry and trouble. Others advise trips, new scenes, new personal associations away from the too-familiar places where it is difficult to escape from disturbing thought vibrations and associations.

I once knew an elderly couple who lost their only son in the Normandy invasion. For months after receiving news of the boy's death, the couple kept his room intact just as it was when he left. On Sundays they would spend hours rearranging the furniture and fondly handling his belongings. With minds so constantly occupied with the memories of their son, was it any wonder that they became embittered old people? I know what it means to lose loved ones, but I have also learned that it is necessary to close the door on yesterday and keep it closed. We live today, not yesterday. As Edgar Allan Poe wrote in "The Premature Burial," "There are moments when, even to the sober eye of Reason, the world of our sad Humanity may assume the semblance of a Hell . . . The grim legion of sepulchral terrors cannot be regarded as altogether fanciful—but . . . they must sleep, or they will devour us—they must be suffered to slumber, or we perish."

Now that you understand how circumstances, environments, and material objectives come into your life through thinking, it's up to you to make your cherished dreams come true.

Suppose you want a new home. After you've got the first glimpse of the picture, start your affirmations going. Use any expressions you wish, or something like this: "I'm going to have that new home. I'm going to have that new home. I'm going to have that new home." And one day, you will find the way, and the new home will be yours.

If you're a salesman and want to increase your sales, use the cards, as already suggested. Tell yourself as frequently as possible that you are going to increase your sales. Do it with emphasis.

Strange as it may sound, we usually get what we anticipate. And if you anticipate increasing your sales and believe that you are going to do it, your sales will mount just as though some invisible friend were helping out. The idea of anticipation holds in everything we do.

One insurance man increased his business more than 200 per cent within a year after he began using this science: "The sales manager told me to call upon Mr. Blank and not come back to the office until I got an order out of him. This prospect was a hard nut to crack. Everyone knew he had the reputation of being very stubborn and cranky with little time for salesmen—to say nothing of us in the insurance business. However, I knew that he had lots of property and had to carry all sorts of fire and liability coverage. As I went down the stairs from our office and all the way up the street to this prospect's office, I kept repeating to myself, 'Fred, you're going to sell him, you're going to sell him. You're going to find him a fine old fellow, no matter what anyone says. He's going to be friendly and he's going to accept what you have to offer.' Maybe I repeated those ideas a couple of hundred times. Not only did he turn out to be very cordial, but I came away with an order for a $25,000 policy, the first our company had ever secured from the old man."

Not long after, this insurance man left the agency he was connected with, opened a firm of his own, rapidly developed a country estate into a showplace, and told me that he was "fixed financially for life."

Dale Carnegie has told of the great success of Howard Thurston, the magician. According to the story, before going out on the stage, Thurston would repeatedly tell himself that he loved his audience and that he was going to give them the best he had in him. He made two million dollars!

Another man—at seventy-eight, he didn't look more than sixty—was a profound student of this subject and used it to make a tremendous fortune for himself. His later interests were along other lines, but he declared that he still ordered his subconscious mind to get busy for him:

"I talk to it just as I might be talking to some individual to whom I was giving orders. And I never have any doubts or fears that it will not do as ordered. If I get an upset stomach, I simply tell it to be itself and act naturally; so with other ailments that arise. If I want to awaken at five o'clock in the morning without using an alarm clock, I peremptorily order my subconscious mind to awaken me. It has never failed in anything so far.

"I have long had a theory that the subconscious mind controls our age—what I mean is that for centuries the subconscious mind has been led to believe that a man should be old when he is sixty. For most people who have accepted the thought, it can't be otherwise, for that is what the subconscious mind believes. However, in my case I refuse to accept it and, as you know, I am as active as I was when I was fifty years old—and I expect to carry on for some years to come."

All of which shows the advisability of not planting in your subconscious mind the idea that you are becoming old and incapable merely because the years are passing. It also shows that by keeping the subconscious free from the fixed idea of a decline, you improve your chances of prolonging your life far beyond the so-called allotted span.

Repetition is the fundamental rhythm of all progress, the cadence of the universe. It's the chuff-chuff of the locomotive that pulls a train across the continent, it's the repeated explosions that generate power in the internal combustion engine. The constant surging of the water against the turbine blades generates electrical power. The tap-tap of the hammer drives the nail into place. The deadly put-put of the machine gun mows down everything before it. Constant and determined effort breaks down all resistance, sweeps away all obstacles. The repeated auto- or heterosuggestion makes you and others believe. The tap-tap of the same conscious thought causes it to be impressed upon your subconscious mind and on the subconscious minds of others.

Anyone can demonstrate the efficacy of the repeated suggestion, whether used constructively or destructively, but Professor Hugo Münsterberg, Harvard psychologist, throws considerable light on its value. He said, "The value of repetition must distinctly be understood in the relation of the inner-setting and the inner mental attitude."

Before World War II there was in Paris a famous institute

devoted to teaching suggestion by means of phonograph records played over and over again.

Listeners could hear any repeated suggestion they wanted—that they were in good health; that they had the power to overcome their difficulties; that they could receive help in other ways.

For years mothers have been taught to talk to their babies and small children while they were asleep, repeating suggestions that they were going to grow well and strong, develop good habits, and become good citizens. Since the children were asleep, the suggestions were obviously directed to their subconscious minds.

In the destruction of Carthage, the greatest maritime city of the ancient world, we have an instance of the power of the repeated suggestion at work. Convinced that Rome and Carthage could not both survive, Cato, the great Roman statesman, ended every speech in the Senate with the words, "Carthage must be destroyed!" He kept it up until the Romans were repeating in their sleep, "Carthage must be destroyed"—and Carthage was.

Many people become confused and frustrated because they let themselves be influenced by others' negative thoughts. This is a weakness of many salesmen, when they absorb too much of what the prospect says about his reasons for not buying. Repetition of negative thoughts, if continued long enough, will discourage even the most powerful. Unless your mind is closed against them and you counteract them by constantly thinking and radiating positive thoughts, sooner or later you will find yourself sunk. Some people wear themselves out trying to combat negative forces by super-human effort and sheer will power, never realizing that their own minds, operating in accordance with the suggestive influences, are causing all the trouble.

Whether we know it or not, we are all victims of suggestion—in many cases almost to the point of being hypnotized. We follow along a beaten path of living just because we've been doing it for decades. For years, houses, churches, office buildings, automobiles, buses, all followed a certain pattern. We wear certain styles of clothing, hold to certain customs, all because we have been led to believe—through the never-ending suggestive thoughts that come to us from all sides—that this is the thing to do. When someone adopts a new way of doing things, he is considered a crank or an eccentric. On close analysis, mass hypnosis can be seen operating in every human activity.

I have observed that those who consciously use this science (as well as those who may be using it unconsciously) are people of tremendous energies, virtually human dynamos. They not only use their imaginations and hold strong beliefs and convictions, but they are great doers in action. And that brings me to a most important statement: "Faith without action is dead."

Unquestionably, there are people on this earth who—without moving from their offices or making any contacts, personal or otherwise, with other people—can achieve remarkable things by concentrated thought. But in the main, this so-called material world of ours is controlled by men of action—those great dynamos of energy who energize others. Nikola Tesla, who probably understood the laws of vibration better than any other man of his time, declared that with a machine that could be slipped into his pocket, he could disintegrate the Empire State Building. (As a matter of fact, when Tesla was first experimenting with a somewhat similar bit of apparatus during the eighteen-nineties, it did cause buildings to shake, windows to break and furniture to move in lower New York.) That machine came out of Tesla's mind. His thoughts created it. There is an example of a man who coupled his "faith with action."

Some metaphysicians and teachers of the occult claim that a person can sit in his own office and visualize orders pouring on to his desk—and the orders will quickly materialize. But to accomplish this, the mental picture or thought projection must be definite and unwavering, and *that* requires great practice and concentration. Stranger things have been recorded, but for the person who has not yet developed this mind-power, it is well to add action and energy to one's efforts by doing the things, following out the ideas, and making the contacts dictated by the subconscious mind.

Many years ago I read that Franklin D. Roosevelt constantly made use of his subconscious mind, and I am certain that he knew much about the use of the repeated suggestion. He never looked backward, but always forward—"yesterday" was a closed book. On April 17, 1945, five days after F.D.R.'s death, Kirke L. Simpson—

an Associated Press Staff Writer and an intimate of the late President—told of a party given Roosevelt after he had been stricken with infantile paralysis.

Roosevelt was determined to walk again, somehow, anyhow, without crutches. According to Mr. Simpson, his intimates decided to give him a cane as a token that they too expected him to walk again, and after it was presented, F.D.R. sat all evening with the cane cuddled against his shoulder. Simpson said that he would reach up to pat its crook now and then, and "we knew that he was saying to himself, 'You'll walk again, Frank Roosevelt; you will walk again!'"

Roosevelt firmly believed in the power of believing. An article in *Time* Magazine for March 4, 1946 told of a letter he wrote in 1924 to a doctor seeking advice on the treatment of infantile paralysis. Mr. Roosevelt pointed out that he thought gentle exercise, massage, and sunbathing were essential. "But," he added, "more important than most therapy is a belief on the patient's part that he will eventually recover." Here we have a wonderful example of the magic of believing at work, and of the part repeated suggestion plays in establishing belief.

chapter six

The mirror technique for releasing the subconscious

The toughest problem that confronts most people is a lack of money. While I have heard of people finding bundles of $1,000 bills by using this Mind Stuff, I think that money comes as a result of combining Mind Stuff and energized action. Certainly your thought can attract money, and once it appears on the horizon, your thought will lead you to ways and means of acquiring it. While I was in the investment banking business, I knew many people of large means and found that every one of them had a "money consciousness." They *thought* wealth, and their coming to possess it was quite similar to my own experience related earlier in this book.

It is always the same technique, no matter what your desires. Get the picture of what you want and keep telling yourself that you're going to get it. But don't think it is going to come to you if you merely indulge in a period of watchful waiting. Go to work, always keeping your goal in mind, and start saving. Every dollar you save out of your weekly paycheck is a step nearer to the fortune that is going to be yours. Consider it as such and save as many dollars as you can. The more you save, the faster you will build that fortune.

Then put your savings out at interest, invest them where they will work advantageously for you, not by gambling or playing the market, but in securities of proven worth, in real estate, or in a business of your own. As your investment grows under your money consciousness, you'll be agreeably surprised to find that the more you have, the more you accumulate. Furthermore, you'll find it exciting and stimulating. Opportunities for profitable investments will come to you from many unexpected and unknown sources, but don't make the mistake that many do and follow will-o'-the-wisps; get sound advice before you invest a cent.

I recall one woman and her daughter who in twenty-five years accumulated more than half a million dollars, largely represented by apartment houses and store buildings. The woman's husband died shortly after World War I, leaving her with a fairly large-sized house. She was at her wits' end how to support herself and her daugher, who had just finished high school. She had had no previous experience in holding a job or carrying on a business, but she could cook and keep house. One morning the idea came to her to take in roomers and boarders.

That was the start, and success came rapidly. Within two years she sold the house and the business, realizing a handsome profit, and then bought a much larger house directly across the street from a well-known men's club, believing that with her high-grade cooking she could get much of the club's overflow business. She did—and prospered; even though she employed plenty of help, no task was too lowly for her in a rush period.

A retired elderly business man who had taken up his home at her place one day suggested that she open a tea room. He said he would provide the necessary funds to fix up a place. She found the top floor of an office building in the business section and opened the tea room. She herself served as hostess, and her daughter was cashier during rush hours, and at other times helping in the kitchen and directing her employees, she soon made the tea room a favorite eating-place for business men. That led to her purchase of a beach hotel through a mortgage company, and also to the profitable sale of the tea room.

All of this time she was investing in securities, and before long she had accumulated a nest egg of $25,000, which went as the first payment on a run-down apartment house. Remodeling under her direction made the building remarkably attractive, and under her management it became very popular. With the great results achieved, her reputation came to the attention of an insurance company that owned other apartment houses, and she was offerd the management of a number of them on a salary and a percentage basis. As her capital grew, her opportunities to buy apartment houses followed, and the last time I heard of this woman with the "money-consciousness," she owned not only apartment houses in this particular city, but had also purchased an apartment house at a nearby beach resort. Before, it had operated only during the summer months, but now she has paying customers all year round.

It has long been my observation that a person with a workable idea seldom has any difficulty in getting money to finance himself. However, he must be thoroughly "sold" on the idea himself before he can convince others to lend him money. If you contemplate having your own business, think about this and use the science of belief, for you'll find someone with money who will help you.

Great fortunes are not built in a day, but come as a result of dollars adding themselves to those you already have or to those you earn and save. But if you want a fortune, you must put your mind and energies to work. It will come—just use the magic of believing.

Here's another case where by using this science, success followed in rapid order—in less than ten years. A corner druggist went into bankruptcy. The fixtures were owned by the owner of the building, a man of considerable wealth, and most of the stock by a wholesale druggist. A young pharmacist heard about the location, but had no funds with which to proceed. Finally the wholesaler and the landlord got together, and the young fellow sold himself to both of them. The landlord, anxious to keep the place occupied, agreed to finance the young fellow for several months and, with necessary guarantees to the wholesaler, the place was reopened. His wife helped behind the counter and at the fountain, and the business began to grow.

For a long time the young druggist had been interested in a preparation which he thought would help people, but he had never had the funds to finance himself. One day he decided to talk with the owner of the building. So thoroughly did he believe in his plan that he had no trouble in convincing the owner, who organized a company for the young fellow and put up $5,000 to start. For months the preparation was bottled in the basement of the druggist's rented home during evenings after the store was closed. People began to buy it in increasing quantities, and the business began to expand. It spread all over the country. Within a few years the landlord was not only paid off, but told me that his profit was better than $50,000. The young fellow's income was now more than $100,000 a year; he and his company now own the building where he started.

In the midst of the so-called Depression, another man told me a remarkable story. He had been in clerical positions most of his life, but one day found himself on the WPA payroll. To get help for some of her troubles, his wife had taken up with a religious organization that insisted upon tithing—that is, upon all members contributing 10 percent of their incomes.

One night his wife prevailed upon this man to accompany her to church, and then "the light hit me," as he told me. Upon arriving home, "something" led him to search for an old formula which his father had used in preparing a lotion that could be used in all barber and beauty shops. Finding the formula, he began visiting junk shops and scrap piles to gather old bottles, which he took home and washed—and they became the first containers. This man went personally from barbershop to barbershop, from beauty parlor to beauty parlor. So convincing were his stories that before long he gave up his WPA job and opened up a plant of his own. He believed thoroughly that the tithing principle was responsible for his good fortune and for all of the ideas that came to him. His product became widely known throughout the country, but the man no longer supplied the trade personally—wholesalers pushed it, and he had his own sales organization as well. Another illustration of the magic of believing.

Thousands of people, particularly the Mormons, are firm believers in tithing, and, one of our greatest industrialists, who preached religion in his own organization and to outsiders, attributed much of his success to the practice of tithing. Another man who was very successful in the selling of baking machines and equipment credited his success entirely to his tithing. I can't say whether this giving of one-tenth of their income to the church or to some religious or charitable organization had anything to do with these individuals' success. But surely these tithers believe thoroughly in the efficacy of their practices, and who is there to say that it doesn't work for them?

Everything on the material plane is first an idea, a thought in someone's mind. A person selling a commodity is actually selling an idea—if it's a machine, what the machine will do; if building material, how it can be used; if food, how nutritious and tasty it will be; and so on endlessly. Every business, every fortune is the outgrowth of an idea, the workings of someone's imagination followed by action.

For years I watched the progress of the Jantzen Knitting Mills, makers of the famous Jantzen swimming suits. I have seen this manufacturing concern grow from practically nothing but an idea to an organization that circles the globe, and the success story of those behind it rivals any told by Horatio Alger. Several times I discussed this science with J. A. Zehntbauer, president of the company and chairman of its board, and with his permission I quote a letter he wrote to me:

> As you say, some people seem to possess an indefinable something which spurs them on to a successful and happy life, while others apparently work hard but without that something in their characters which brings them satisfaction and success.
>
> I have never tried systematically to develop this indefinable spirit, but believe it has been developed in me by my parents, and especially by my mother. There were four youngsters in our family, three boys and one girl. She promptly fought our inclination to say, "I can't do this" or "I can't do that," by telling us that of course, we can do anything anyone else can do.
>
> All that was necessary was to tackle the job and keep on trying until it was mastered—and we would then be ready to tackle a bigger job—and to shrink from no job because it was great or unimportant. She was constantly resisting our inclination to complain or growl about anything. When we were in a complaining disposition, she would say, "Don't grumble but think what a privilege it is to live in such a wonderful world. Instead of complaining, brace right up and keep smiling and enjoy the blessings at hand."
>
> We have always been exceptionally happy, and I attribute it to the training of our parents. Mother, with her constant training, and Father corroborating her often by saying, "Always look on the bright side, never on the dark side of things."
>
> If one has not been fortunate enough to have the advantages of such influ-

ences, I can see it would take a great amount of self-discipline and training to
bring one up to the point of view which, you clearly point out, is necessary to
get the most out of life. Regardless of one's present circumstances, I am sure
the application of your science would be valuable to him.

In today's business world, the competition is unusually keen. Naturally, the person best prepared for a certain position is in a far better situation to get it. I do not wish to give the idea that a man with neither education nor experience can step out of a job in an industrial plant and immediately take over the reins of a large corporation simply by using this science of belief. There may be exceptional cases of men doing this, but they are few and far between.

First things always come first, and if a man feels entitled to a better job and has prepared himself for it, then the use of this science can get him that job, or one even better.

A well-known executive once said to me, "The difficulty I see with most people seeking employment is that they are so wrapped up in themselves that they make no effort to impress their prospective employer with what they can do to help him, overlooking the fact that the other fellow is only interested in you to the extent that you can help him." This may appear a cold-blooded attitude to some readers, but in the world of competition, self-interest is a reality that all job-hunters must face.

There is an old saying that if you do not follow your own thoughts, then you will follow the thoughts of the fellow who followed his. It means exactly what it says—it marks the difference between a leader and a follower. Those who don't think and use their creative abilities are always being given orders by those who do. Unless you are willing to think, you will have to labor physically, and this means you will receive less pay for your work.

Therefore, visualize the kind of job you want. Use your cards and your constant affirmations until belief in your goal becomes a vital part of you, and you feel it in your blood, your bones, and in every tissue of your body. See yourself actually doing the things you visualize, and it will all work out, because every thought held constantly and persistently sooner or later materializes after its kind.

Everyone has taken a vacation trip at sometime or another. Did you ever stop to analyze the mental processes involved? First you got the idea of the trip. Then you decided where you would go. Shortly you began to visualize yourself in the mountains, at the seashore, or visiting some new city. The vacation turned out as planned because you saw yourself doing it—before the trip actually became a reality. Could anything be clearer? Whatever you want to do, just apply the same principles, and you will get the same successful results.

You will remember the card device, which I explained in detail. Before explaining another device, which I call the mirror technique, let me tell you how I happened to discover this truly wonderful thing and how it can be used to bring quicker and more effective results.

Many years ago, I was the guest of a very wealthy man who owned many patents for logging and sawmill machinery. He invited a number of newspaper publishers, bankers, and industrial leaders to his suite in a prominent hotel to explain a new method he had devised for mill operations. Liquor flowed freely, and soon the host himself was very much intoxicated.

Just before dinner was served, I saw him stagger into his bedroom and pull himself up abruptly before his dresser. Thinking that I might help him, I followed him to the door of his room. As I stood there, he grabbed the edge of the dresser top with both hands and stared into the mirror, mumbling as a drunken man sometimes does. Then his words began to make sense, and I moved back a little to watch. I heard him say: "John, you old son-of-a-gun, they tried to get you drunk, but you're going to fool them. You're sober, you're sober, cold sober. This is your party, and you've got to be sober."

As he kept repeating these words, while continuing to stare at his reflection in the mirror, I noticed a transfiguration taking place. His body was becoming more erect, the muscles of his face were tightening, and his drunken look was disappearing. The whole performance was over in perhaps five minutes.

In my experience as a newspaper man and a police reporter, I had observed many drunken people, but never had I seen such a rapid change. Not wanting him to know I had observed him, I made for the bathroom. When I got back to the dining room, I found our host at the head of the table. While his face was still a little flushed, to all appearances he was sober. At the end of the dinner he presented a very dramatic and convincing picture of his new plans. Not until long afterward, when I got a better understanding of the power of the subconscious mind, did I understand the science involved in transforming that obviously drunken man into a cold-sober host.

I have given the mirror technique to thousands of people, with some very unusual results. Over the years a large number of people came to me for help with their problems. A surprising number were women, and practically all of them started their stories with weeping spells. The first thing I did was to stand them before a full length mirror and have them take a good look at themselves; I made them look into their eyes and tell me what they saw there—crybabies or fighters? Their crying soon ceased, and those cases convinced me that a woman cannot weep while looking at herself in a mirror. Whether pride, shame, or repudiating the idea that they are weaklings stops them short, the fact remains that the tears stop flowing.

Many great orators, preachers, actors, and statesmen have used the mirror technique. According to Drew Pearson, Winston Churchill never made a speech of importance unless he made it before a mirror first. Pearson also declared that Woodrow Wilson employed the same technique. It's what I call a supercharging method of stepping up the speaker's subconscious forces so that when he appears before an audience, those forces flow out to and affect his listeners. By using the mirror in rehearsing the speech as you are going to deliver it, you are creating a picture of yourself, your words, the sound of your voice, and your sight of the audience, to which the immediate future is to bring reality. By looking into the mirror, you increase the mental vibrations by which the force and meaning of your words will quickly penetrate to your audience's subconscious minds.

This mirror technique gives a possible clue to the power and personal magnetism of certain evangelists. I knew Bill Sunday in his heyday and often heard him preach, but in those days, knowing little or nothing about this Mind Stuff, I was puzzled as to how he and other great evangelists were able to influence people to such a remarkable degree.

However, we now have proof that Billy Sunday was versed in the use of the mirror technique; it was given by Eric Sevareid in his book *Not So Wild a Dream*, published in 1946. Mr. Sevareid tells how

he as a young newspaper reporter secured an interview with Billy
Sunday.

*He bounded about the hotel room, now peering intently out of the window,
with one foot on the sill, now grasping the dressing-table firmly in both hands
while lecturing his reflection in the mirror.*

Early on, one of the most outstanding insurance salesmen in
America accepted the science of belief. He told me that he never
called upon an important prospect without first giving his sales
presentation in front of a mirror. His sales were phenomenal.

Every salesman has heard the statement, "If you can convince
yourself, you can convince the other fellow"—which is basically
true. Every great mass movement in history, from religious to mili-
tary, has come about through an individual whose flaming belief in
his own cause gave him the power to convert thousands of others. A
man need not study psychology to know that enthusiasm is contagious and that someone bursting with it can readily transmit it to
others. The mirror technique is a simple and effective method by
which you can strengthen your belief in your own sales ability and
thus intensify the power of your enthusiasm.

Whether we know it or not, we're all engaged in selling
something—if not our wares, then our personalities, services, or
ideas. As a matter of fact, all human relationships are based upon
selling of one kind or another, and we all engage in it whenever we
try to persuade others to our way of thinking. Legally, a contract or
agreement is based on a meeting of the minds, and unless you can
get the other person to think your way, you do not get very far. But
once the minds meet on the major issues, the rest is easy, and the
name on the dotted line is but a matter of a few more moments.

When considered in the light of the science given in this book,
the mirror technique becomes a master method by which the subconscious mind's mighty forces can be employed to influence those
you're dealing with. During the "Depression" days, when I was
working with many sales organizations to increase their business, I
introduced this mirror method with some startling results. I had
mirrors fastened to the inside back doors in all of a pie-baking
company's trucks, so that when the driver-salesmen opened the

doors to get their goods for delivery, those mirrors were the first thing they saw. I always admonished each man that before calling on a customer, he should determine how many pies he was going to sell, and then tell himself in the mirror that he would leave that number of pies on his customer's counter. One driver told me that he had been trying to sell one woman restaurant owner for many months, but she had always refused to buy any pies. Then he decided to try the mirror technique. That day he sold her ten pies. At the time he told me his story he was selling her an average of fifteen pies a day.

The mirror technique was used with great effectiveness in insurance companies, financial houses, rubber mills, automobile agencies, cookie manufacturing plants, and many other organizations with salesmen or production operators. In my own old organization, where we had to make a complete about-face to avert disaster, I first used this technique by placing a mirror in a back room of the office where the employees left their hats and overcoats. It was so placed that everyone had to see it when entering or leaving the room. At first I pasted strips of paper with such slogans as "We're going to win," "Nothing is impossible to an indefatigable mind," "We've got the guts, let's prove it," "Let's show the world we're not licked and then go to town," "How many are you going to sell today?" and a great many others. We later took to using soap to write the slogans directly on the face of the mirror.

Every morning a new slogan appeared, with the sole purpose of convincing our employees that they could get business, even though other firms in the same line were struggling to keep their doors open. Later this setup was augmented by a second mirror alongside the door-frame of the main door to the office, which would always be the last thing the salesmen saw as they left.

Subsequently I placed mirrors alongside calendar frames on the desks of all salesmen and executives. The startling thing about it was that during the worst of the "Depression" days the salesmen— and I mean *all* of them—trebled and quadrupled their incomes, and they maintained their progress ever since. A number of men whose monthly income probably never exceeded $300 in the best of times now averaged better than $1,000 a month. This may sound incredible, but it's true. In my files are many letters from executives, salesmen, and others who have testified to the effectiveness of the mirror idea.

Now to outline the technique.

Stand in front of a mirror. It need not be full-length, but it should be large enough so that you can at least see your body from the waist up.

Those of you who have been in the Army know what it means to come to attention—stand fully erect, bring your heels together, pull in your stomach, keep your chest out and your head up. Now breathe deeply three or four times until you feel a sense of power, strength, and determination. Next, look into the very depths of your eyes, tell yourself that you are going to get what you want—name it aloud so you can see your lips move and hear the words uttered.

Make a regular ritual of it, practice doing it at least twice a day, mornings and evenings—and you will be surprised at the results. You can augment this by writing with soap on the face of the mirror any slogans or key words you wish, so long as they are the key to what you have visualized before and want to see in reality. Within a few days, you will have developed a sense of confidence that you never realized you could build within yourself.

If you are planning to call on an exceptionally tough prospect or are proposing to interview the boss whom you may have previously feared, use the mirror technique and keep it up until you are convinced that you can make the proper presentation without any trepidation. And if you are called upon to make a speech, by all means practice before a mirror. Gesticulate, pound your fist on the palm of your other hand to drive home the arguments—use any other gestures that come naturally to you.

As you stand before the mirror, keep telling yourself that you are going to be an outstanding success and that nothing in this world is going to stop you. Does this sound silly? Don't forget that every idea presented to the subconscious mind is going to produce its exact counterpart in objective life, and the quicker your subconscious gets the idea, the sooner your wish becomes a picture of power. Certainly it is not good business for you to tell anyone of the devices you employ, because scoffers might ridicule you and shake your confidence, especially if you are just beginning to learn the science.

If you are an executive or sales manager and want to put more push into your entire organization, teach your employees the mirror technique and see that they use it, just as many organizations now do.

Much has been written about the power of the eyes. The eyes are said to be the windows of the soul; they reveal your thoughts. They express you far more than you imagine. They permit others to "get your number," as the saying goes. You will find, however, that once you start this mirror practice, your eyes will take on a power that you never realized you could develop (something that writers have referred to as a dynamic or fascinating power). This will give you that penetrating gaze that makes others think you are looking into their very souls. Sooner or later will come an intensity to bespeak the intensity of your thought, which people will begin to recognize. Emerson wrote that every man carries in his eye the exact indication of his rank. Remember that your own gradation or position in life is marked by what you carry in your eyes. So develop eyes that bespeak confidence. The mirror will help you.

This mirror technique may be used in many different ways, and with very gratifying results. If you have a poor posture, or are slovenly in your walk, you will find that practice before a full-length mirror will work wonders. Your mirror shows you the person others see when they look at you, and you can fashion yourself into any kind of person you would like them to see.

It is said that if you act the part you will become that part, and here again, there is no better way than rehearsing your act before the mirror. Vanity has no part in this science. Consequently, don't use the mirror in a supercilious manner, but use it to build yourself into the person you wish to be. If some of the world's most outstanding men and women use this mirror technique to build themselves and increase their influence over other people, surely you can use it for your own special requirements.

Much has been written about intuition and hunches. Some psychologists claim that the ideas which come to us intuitively are not something "out of the blue," but arise as a result of our accumulated knowledge or as echoes of something we may have seen or heard before. That may be true to some extent with chemists, inventors, and others who work by the trial-and-error method, using their prior knowledge and the results of previous experiments. But I believe that by far the greatest number of discoveries, illuminations, and inspired works come direct from the subconscious mind, and are not syntheses of previous knowledge that's been filed away. Every custom we follow, everything we utilize was first an idea in someone's mind, and that idea came first in the way of a hunch, an intuitive flash, or call it what you will. So it is wise to heed your own intuitions and to trust them to the end.

Many great leaders, industrialists, and inventors have openly admitted following the hunches that came to them in odd moments of relaxation or in periods when they were engaged in some task other than trying to solve their problems. A good way to prompt your subconscious mind is for you to tackle a problem from all angles consciously. Then some night, just before dropping off to sleep, order your subconscious mind to bring you the answer. You may awaken in the middle of the night, or the answer may come to you upon awakening in the morning or at some odd moment the next day when you are engaged in something quite different. Be quick to grasp it when it comes, and waste no time in following through with it.

You may have a hunch to visit or telephone a certain man. He may be the head of some concern and may well be of great help to you. Because of his position, however, you may fear to make the move; you struggle with your "hunch" on one hand and your fear on the other. Too often, the fear wins. The next time fear or doubt enters your mind, ask yourself this question: "What have I got to lose if I *do* see him or call him? What harm can it do?" Your fears and doubts can't answer that question! So obey your hunch without delay.

A word of warning should be given here, however. Many people like to gamble. Some play cards, others bet on the horse or dog races, and many play the stock market. Undoubtedly you have heard people say that now and then they follow their hunches and make a killing. But I urge you not to use your hunches in an endeavor to get something for nothing. There seems to be something fundamentally wrong about it, because most gamblers die broke. Also, beware of hunches that would lead you into untried fields. They may not be intuition at all, but just sudden fanciful longings. The *true* kind of hunch is always concerned with something already related to you directly or indirectly, and it gives you the idea and the momentum to carry out the necessary action.

I take it for granted that none of my readers will assume this book to be an open-sesame to overnight riches and fame. It is intended only as a key to unlock the door that opens on the road leading to any goal you desire. Certainly it wouldn't be wise to rush into undertakings far beyond your present capabilities or development. If you would be the head of a great utility concern, naturally you would have to learn the business, just as if you aspired to become head of a huge transportation system. But by using this science, you can learn the various steps that will take you to the top. However, before any program is undertaken, you must have a plan of action. You wouldn't go to the corner drugstore and just ask for drugs. You'd be specific and name the brand of aspirin you wanted. And so it is with this science—you've got to know what you want and be specific about it.

If you have definitely determined what you want and have fixed yourself a goal, then consider yourself extremely fortunate—you have taken the first step that will lead to success! As long as you hold on to the mental picture of your idea and begin to develop it with action, nothing can stop you from succeeding, for the subconscious mind never fails to obey any order given clearly and emphatically.

chapter
seven

How to project
your thoughts

Success is a matter of never-ceasing application. You must work at it diligently, or else it takes wings and flies away. At no time can you afford to rest on your laurels or pause for self-admiration, because others may be coveting your place and would love to push you out of it, especially if they observe that you have a weak hold or are doing anything to strengthen your position.

Despite the great strides that America has made, this country still has many great resources that haven't yet been tapped. Computers, genetic engineering, micro-surgery, organ transplants, digital recording, laser surgery, and the hi-tech Space Shuttle program have all opened up hitherto-unexplored fields. But I can confidently believe that we haven't seen anything yet, that still greater things will be accomplished by men and women with imaginations and the will-to-do. Those of us who are still alive 50 years from now may well be looking on a world that makes the late 20th century seem as the Industrial Revolution does today.

As late as 1948, laboratory scientists were working on what many at the time considered fantastic ideas—including wearable fabrics made from wood fiber, materials that would be water and fire-resistant, machines that would capture energy from the sun, and even apparatus that would record our unspoken fears and anxieties on a graph. All these "miracles," now quite commonplace, came from men and women's imaginations or from their subconscious minds. Perhaps in less than fifty years, thought-transference or telepathy will be as commonplace as the radio of today. Who knows?

It has been said that man can materialize anything that he can conceive of mentally, and the millions of devices we use and enjoy today prove it. When man fully comprehends the great power of his mind and earnestly puts it to work, he will have dominion over not only this earth and everything on it, but he may reach out to control the nearby planets. You yourself have this inner spark, but you must fan it until the fire is white-hot and you must constantly stoke it, which you do by adding fuel—ideas, ideas, more ideas, and action.

One man I knew who had many achievements to his credit—and who was over seventy—declared that most people fall by the wayside because they are never starting anything. "I make a plan, and have for years, to start something new—new for me—at least once a week. It may only be making some simple gadget to use in the kitchen, or it may be an entirely new sales plan or reading an unfamiliar book. In following this plan, I not only keep my body and mind active, but also I put to use a lot of imaginative qualities that otherwise might fall asleep and atrophy. To me, the idea of a man's retiring when he's sixty-five is a great mistake. As soon as a man retires and quits being active, mentally and physically, he's on the way to his grave in short order. You have seen what has happened to horses when they are retired. You know what happens to your automobile when you leave it outside unused and neglected; it starts to rust and is soon headed for the junk shop. Humans are the same; when they go on the shelf, they rust out or wither and die."

The plan of starting something new at least once a week brings us to the matter of how valuable individual initiative is for any person who seeks success. Without it, a man is stopped as soon as he starts. Men and women remain in minor clerical positions all their lives because they never display initiative in their work, never attempt to find new ways of doing it, and never suggest improvements.

During World War II, a number of organizations placed suggestion boxes in their plants and offered prizes for the most practical. Frequently these suggestions led to greatly improved methods in plant operations, as well as rewards in advancement for the employees offering the suggestions. In a number of instances, suggestions led to patentable devices that brought fame and fortune to those employees supplying the initial ideas. Bear in mind that no matter how long a piece of work has been done in a certain way, there's always a better way—the war demonstrated that.

So give heed to initiative. Even if you are just a clerk behind the counter in some store, you must have some ideas of how goods can be better displayed or how the customers can be better served. Good ideas for lighting, color schemes, arrangement of the counters and display shelves are always acceptable to management, and are often rewarded.

Closely linked with initiative are interest and attention. The more interest you take in your work, naturally the more attention you give it and the greater the results. We all do best what interests us, so if the task before you does not interest you, look for one that will. The more absorbing the interest, the better—that factor alone will give you momentum and carry you a long way forward.

One woman I knew was employed as assistant to the manager of a large department store. Although her salary was fixed under the war-time ceiling, for several years she received the store's highest Christmas bonus because of her interest and initiative. The head of the store often sought her advice, rather than the manager's.

The personnel manager of a huge defense plant employing many thousands of men and women told me that the greatest fault he found in people was that he could not depend upon them. Some fail to keep their word, others are always late for their engagements, still others are forever changing their minds. So if you tell someone else that you are going to do a certain thing, do it even though its fulfillment may cause you some inconvenience, no matter what the consequences or the cost in time or energy. You will be amply repaid, for building a reputation for reliability will be of great value to you as you proceed up the ladder.

Many employees hold to the idea that their work is given to them merely to further their employers' interests. They never entertain the thought that they are actually working for themselves, with the employer merely furnishing the tools and a place for them to work. There is an old saying that unless a man has learned to take orders, he can never learn to give them. How true this is, but few people, working day after day, ever realize it is within their own power to sit some day in the executive's place and give orders.

"The only way to have a friend is to be one," said Emerson, but few ever give thought to this fundamental requirement. You can't cast your bread upon the waters without having it returned, and you can't do a good deed without having a good deed done to you in return. This is true, no matter how Pollyanna-ish it may sound to some people.

Rare indeed is the man who doesn't make an enemy now and then. You get out of tune with a man, or perhaps he gets out of tune with you. Naturally, you don't like him; as a result of your thinking, he doesn't like you. Fortunate is he who is able to make a friend of that enemy—and it's so easily done. Several men have taken a violent dislike to me, perhaps because of something I may have said in an unguarded moment, and would have figuratively liked to cut my throat. But they have become my staunchest friends merely by my thinking and believing that they were really friendly people.

I don't know whether the idea of converting enemies into friends came to me out of the blue, whether I read it, or whether someone told me. But it has been part of my creed for years, and I've always found it to work. For example an executive who had taken a dislike to me for something I said critically about his company's operations. For months, he was profanely knocking me at every opportunity. Naturally, my first impulse was to fight back and knock him in return. But the day came when I realized that his enmity had resulted from something I had said about *him* rather than the company.

"He's not a bad guy," I said to myself. "I'm wrong. I started the feud, and I'm sorry. The next time I get near him, I am going to tell him that mentally." One night I met him in a club of which we were both members. He would have avoided me, but we met nearly face to face, and I spoke first, saying, "How are you, Charlie?" He caught "something" from my voice that meant a gesture of friendliness on my part, and immediately responded in the friendliest of manners. Today we're the closest of friends.

So remember, some of your enemies may be of your own making. Those friends or enemies are merely a reflection of our own thoughts—the other fellow will consider us an enemy or friend according entirely to the picture which we ourselves conjure up. Only today, as I write this I had an example of this kind of thought projection. The waste pipe of my laundry sink had clogged, and I had to call a plumber. A few blocks from our home was a plumbing shop, whose proprietor was unfriendly and offensive in his treatment of customers.

Several times I had tried to get him to do work for us, but he was always too busy. The last time I had called him, he told me that I would have to wait my turn—probably he could get around to fix up the water heater in a couple of weeks. I had asked if he could give me the names of other plumbers who might help me, but he had been entirely uncooperative. Naturally, his unfriendly treatment gave me a bad impression of plumbers in general, and I found myself damning all of them.

However, I had to get the heater repaired and I quickly realized that my angry attitude toward plumbers engendered by this experience would cause me to have difficulty in obtaining the services of any one of them. I simply changed my thought, saying something like this to myself, "All plumbers are good fellows—the guy you called is just an old grouch—forget it."

I called a friend, the manager of a wholesale plumbing house. He suggested a plumber who would help me, and I telephoned Mr. Jones at once. He said he was busy, but if an imperative job had to be done, he would be out immediately.

His promise pleased me, and the plumber immediately felt my gratitude when he entered our home, fifteen minutes after my call. In less than two hours—he worked swiftly, unlike some plumbers I had employed—the heater had been replaced. I was genuinely delighted by his service and told him so. Naturally that pleased him.

Today it was a little before 8 A.M. when I called him again for help. I reminded the plumber who I was, and that he had been the one who had fixed my water heater. He remembered me immediately and said he'd be out as soon as possible—probably around noon. Within five minutes after I hung up the telephone, a man appeared at the front door, asking if I had called a plumber.

I asked him how come he was on the job so soon when his boss had just told me that he couldn't send a man before noon, and he replied, "Mr. Jones had just received your call as I came into the shop, and he told me to come up to your home and do what was necessary before I went out on my all-day job."

I was elated with this treatment and told the plumber so, which, of course, pleased him. With my help, he repaired the waste pipe in less than half an hour. I told him of my previous experience with the old plumber and his own boss, Mr. Jones.

"My boss is a fine fellow," he replied. "He's always putting himself out to help people and he's building a huge business as a result. Never have I found a better boss."

If you wager, think and believe that the other fellow is a fine chap, that's what he'll turn out to be—for never forget that what you get back is a reflection of what you project mentally.

Do not reject this great truth. Just apply it and you'll be amazed at the startling results. Watch the bus driver respond, the elevator operator beam, and the clerk behind the counter hurry to oblige you when you send out friendly thoughts. It can be used in every encounter in life, and if you're wholly sincere about it, you will never have to worry about making enemies.

"And as ye would that men should do to you, do ye also to them likewise," says the Bible. Many successful men and women, irrespective of any motive that may activate them, work on the assumption that when they do something for another person, something will be done for them. That may sound rather calculating, but the basic law of reciprocity remains, regardless of the situation or circumstances. Simply, there must be a logical effect from every cause.

Doing something for others always pays dividends in one form or another. When you try to please the boss, it isn't a matter of bootlicking. It's just common sense to make him a friend, for in any organization, the people who get ahead do their work well and try to please the boss. The boss does the promoting, and the more pleased he is with you and your work, the faster is your own progress. No matter how great your self-esteem, if you expect progress in any large organization, you must not only do your work well, but you must have the boss's good will. Look around a bit and you'll see this principle at work everywhere. You saw it work in the schoolroom when you were young, you see it at work in the Army, you see it in American politics, and if you have studied animal life, you have recognized it working among the highest and the lowest species.

Take the initiative. Always try to do something for the other fellow, and you will be agreeably surprised how things come your way, how many pleasant things are done for you.

You can experiment for yourself with your dog. Pet him and be kind to him, and his tail will wag in grateful appreciation. He'll try to lick your hand or your face if you'll give him a chance. Scold him or strike him and he may cringe, snarl, or even try to bite you. The reactions of people are similar, and no matter what motivates you to do something for the other person—whether merely a friendly impulse or your own knowledge of the law of cause and effect—the results will be the same.

Sincere compliments will always gain you friends, for most people are extremely susceptible to compliments. Compliments gratify their ego, and up you go in their friendly estimation. Early in their careers, successful politicians learn the art of making friends by doing things for others and speaking in praise of them. The paper boy you befriend today may some day be the policeman who stops you when you have violated some traffic rule, and then you will discover what it means to have a friend at court. The same principle applies in all walks of life, yet many people overlook it.

Not long ago, I was sitting in the office of the merchandise manager of one of the largest department stores in the country when in came a woman employee to thank him for some advice he'd given her about accepting a better position in another city. When she left, he said, "You know, one thing I like about this job is the number of people who come to me for advice. While my job here keeps me on the run, I always take time off for employees who come to me for advice. It flatters me and makes me feel as though I'm quite a fellow, and naturally I feel like doing everything I can for people who compliment me."

This brings me to another point—a person who desires riches must go where riches are. Alone on a desert island, a man would probably have a tough time eking out an existence, to say nothing of trying to amass a fortune. So it is in everyday pursuits. Therefore, if you want money, you've got to associate yourself with people who have it or who know how to make it. This may sound rather crass. But the truth is that if you are after money, you must go where it's being spent. Also, you must become personally acquainted with those who have the authority to spend it. If you are selling advertising and know that the head of the firm is the man with the final say, don't waste your time trying to convince minor clerks and junior executives. The same holds true if you are trying to sell other commodities or—what is more important—yourself.

"If you work for a man, for goodness' sake work for him," said Elbert Hubbard. That brings me to a failing of many people I have worked with over a period of years—lack of interest in their jobs. They make no effort to learn anything outside the small sphere in which their work places them. Once I made a bet with the executive of a large concern whose name was frequently in the newspapers that I could find at least twenty people in his own local organization who had never heard of him or the position he occupied. Not only did he lose the bet, but his pride was hurt when he got the proof. Curiosity prompted me to check with other nation-wide organizations, and not a single employee could tell me the name of the head of the company or the street address of its main office.

This may sound unbelievable, even ridiculous. But if you have friends working in a minor capacity with some large institution, ask them the name of their treasurer or senior vice-president. Unless the company publishes a house organ or employee newsletter, the ignorance will surprise you. Many people accept positions and make no attempt to learn anything about what the adjacent department manufactures or even about the company's general operations. Perhaps the heads of big organizations err in not carrying on educational campaigns for the benefit of employees.

Of course, there are large corporations that have house organs containing the names of the executives and main office locations, giving details about their method of operation. Yet I talked with a woman who had been employed by a large manufacturing plant for many months. Outside of the name of the personnel manager who had hired her, she did not know the name of a single executive of the company in spite of the fact that the company's publication with articles written by various department heads went into her hands every month.

The job you now hold is the steppingstone to the job above it. Before you start moving toward it, how much do you know about it—just how much do you know about your company and its policies both inside and out? If you are a salesman for a major oil company or even a telephone operator, within a short time after your employment you should surely learn the names of the men who head the company and something of their history. Many firms carry group insurance, with the employees paying a small part of the premiums. How many employees ever read their policies? Few do, and, further, few know anything about their Social Security rights or what the various deductions taken from their payroll checks actually represent.

"Man is heir to the wisdom of the ages found within the covers of great books," remarked one of our great wise men, and yet it is surprising how many people never read a book. Strange as it may sound, very few businessmen read anything besides the newspapers and a few trade journals. Professional men more or less limit themselves to books and literature dealing with their respective fields. I mention books, for no matter what it may be—biography, fiction, history, or a scientific text—it is a rare book that doesn't contain an idea or two useful in your own work. No one has a monopoly of knowledge, but we all know that knowledge is power when put to use. The more you read, the more your thinking is stimulated, and if you are a person of action, the more your efforts are accelerated.

Now is the time to mention the highly interesting phenomenon of idea association and how one idea quickly links itself with another. This is of great value and should be cultivated by everyone, especially by people engaged in creative work such as advertising, writing, or selling.

For example, think of an automobile. Consider for a moment how many ideas can be derived from the mental picture of the automobile. It's made of steel, alloys and plastics—each furnishing major ideas that can be broken up into many others. Then consider the wheels and tires—casings, the hubcaps, the valves—all bringing further associations. Think of the roads over which they have traveled, and their construction. Then think of oil and gasoline, which brings further ideas through association. Before we know it, you have started a seemingly endless association of ideas.

Let's take a single idea in business. Suppose you are interested in the growth and sale of a new strain of orange. The first question naturally is: Can it be grown and sold at a profit? Naturally, association of ideas will lead you to determine all matters dealing with soil, location, climatic conditions, costs, labor problems; these will lead on to marketing programs, packaging, dealers who would be interested, brokers, shippers, and finally, the ultimate consumer. The field of ideas becomes enormous through association started with the thought of a single orange.

I should say a word about packaging and eye-appeal, because here again we deal with the power of suggestion. Dealers in groceries, fruits, and garden vegetables know that even if there is no improvement in the products themselves, artistic, attractive-looking packages will bring a better price. To discover this fact for yourself, you have only to stroll through a grocery store and note the articles that attract your attention. Excellence in packaging distinguishes the skilled chef from the ordinary restaurant cook. The expert chef knows the value of eye-appeal and accordingly arranges food on the platters to give it a more appetizing look, while the average short-order cook, probably neither knowing nor caring, piles it on in any old fashion.

For several years I owned a celery farm. My renter, a slovenly fellow, was always complaining that he could not compete with the Japanese and gave this as an excuse for not being able to fulfill his rent contracts. Intuitively, the Japanese knew the value of proper packaging. Their celery would be thoroughly washed, placed in new crates, and if sold in the form of hearts, would frequently be attractively wrapped in paper carrying a boastful little message about the quality of the celery. My renter never, in my memory, washed a single bunch of celery. He packed it in second-hand crates and then complained that his Japanese competitors were getting all the business.

Anyone who has traveled through the great farming belts of the Midwest and Canada can tell by a glance at the house or barn whether the farmer is alive or whether he is dying on his feet. In 1910, some of the great orchardists of the Pacific Northwest couldn't sell a whole wagonload of pears or apples for twenty dollars. Yet in the 1940s, men who had the idea of attractive packaging and marketing made large fortunes. It's nothing to get people to pay two dollars or more for a dozen apples or pears carefully wrapped in tissue paper. Some alert orchardists sell their products by mail to thousands of buyers throughout the world. I happen to know a number of these operators personally, and their success in each instance has been predicated upon an idea that came to them in a flash and which developed as a result of their believing.

Now consider this matter of packaging in connection with yourself. Do you have eye-appeal? Do you wear clothes to give yourself the best appearance? Do you know the effect of colors and study those which best suit your form and temperament? Does your whole appearance set you apart from many who pass unnoticed in the crowd? If not, give thoughtful attention to personal packaging, for the world accepts you as you appear to be. Take a tip from the automobile manufacturers, Hollywood make-up artists, and any of the great restaurant owners, who all know the value of eye-appeal and package their goods accordingly. When you have proper packaging and highest quality goods within, you have an unbeatable combination. The *you* within can do the same thing for the outside *you*—and you too will have the unbeatable combination.

To satisfy yourself on what the right appearance for you really is, just pass by where there is construction under way. If you are well-dressed and have an air of prosperity and importance, workmen in your path will step aside. Or you might step into an outer office where others may be waiting to see a certain executive. Notice that the important-looking individual with the air and voice of authority gets first attention, not only from the office attendants but from the executive.

No better example of the impressiveness of a good appearance can be given than the distinction made among defendants at a police station. The stylishly dressed, well-poised businessman is seldom ill-treated, while the man who looks like a bum lands almost immediately in a cell. As a police reporter on metropolitan newspapers for a number of years, I saw this happen countless times. The fellow who looked as though he might be somebody and who had been arrested for a minor infraction, often got a chair in the captain's office until he could telephone a lawyer or some friend to obtain his release, while the low-life type was carted off to jail, to get his release when and if he could.

The head of a huge automobile distributing agency told me that he was frequently called upon to close a sale with wealthy men who always bought the most expensive cars. "Not only do I take a shower," he said, "and change all my clothes, but I go to a barbershop and get everything from a shave to a shampoo and manicure. Obviously, it has something to do with my appearance, but further than that, it does something to me inside—it makes me feel like a new man who could lick his weight in wildcats."

If you are properly attired when you start out on some important undertaking, you will feel within yourself that sense of power, which will make people give way before you and even stir others to help you on your way. The right mental attitude, keeping your eyes fixed on your goal, and throwing around you the proper aura—which is done by an act of imagination or an extension of your personal magnetism—will work wonders, as Theos Bernard learned when he was cornered and stoned by a crowd of natives in Tibet. In his book *Penthouse of the Gods,* he says that his first reaction was to fight, but immediately dismissed the thought when he recalled having been taught to assume and maintain his own aura. Thus he straightened his shoulders, lifted his head high, directed his eyes straight ahead, and moved forward with a firm and rapid stride. Not only did the crowd give way, but others came forward and made a path for him.

A number of years ago I was friendly with the chief of a large metropolitan fire department. This middle-aged man seemed to fear nothing. Once, I told him that his associates declared he led a charmed life, and he laughed. "I don't know as you'd call it that. Maybe I'm somewhat of a fatalist, but I've never believed that I would be killed as long as I'm chief. When I go into a place of danger, I always throw a white circle about myself, and nothing can come through that circle. It was a trick I learned from the Indians who lived near us when I was a kid. Maybe it's the worst kind of superstition, but that white aura has saved my life more times than I like to think about." He lived to retire and died in his seventies—from natural causes.

Many baseball fans know how the great Babe Ruth "called the shots." If he wanted to hit a home run into right or left field, that's where he batted the ball. How he did this is perhaps known only to that great hero of all American boys, but surely it was uncanny. Against the mightiest pitchers he was able to bat the ball where he wanted, and his home-run record is something that stood for a long time.

Ernie Pyle, the famous war correspondent, experienced a premonition of death. When he left for the Pacific Theater, Ernie had the feeling that he would not return. On the other hand, many ex-servicemen told of having the feeling or belief that they were going to come through intense fire without being wounded—and come through they did. You will find that many people subjected to great danger believe in the efficacy of this white circle or aura. Perhaps here again, it is the result of the magic of believing. Throughout the world, millions of automobile owners keep a small St. Christopher medal in their cars which they believe will save them from accidents. But why stop there?

The vibrations set up by others affect us much more than we realize, for we take on the characteristics of those with whom we associate more or less constantly. After long years together, a man and wife frequently grow to resemble one another and acquire many of one another's habits. A baby will take on the emotional characteristics of the mother or the person who habitually cares for it, becoming susceptible to the same fears, likes and dislikes—and frequently these emotional qualities remain for life. Lovers of pets, especially of dogs, declare that animals take on some of their owners' emotional characteristics—they will be ugly, friendly, happy, or quarrelsome, depending on the emotional pattern of the human with whom they associate most closely.

It is always important to remember that a negative person can raise havoc. In an organization or home, a strong negative personality can do the same amount of damage as a positive personality can do good; and when the two are pitted against one another, the negative frequently becomes the more powerful. We all know what happens to a man living among uncivilized people—occasionally he goes native. Englishmen employed as plantation or mine operators in jungle outposts used to guard against this by shaving and meticulously dressing for dinner each evening.

To have a smoothly running organization, all its members must be attuned to the thinking of the principal executive. Thus an extremely nervous person in a position of authority can put nearly every co-worker into a nervous state. You can see this happen in almost any office or shop where the executive is of a nervous type. Sometimes this emotional pattern will extend throughout an entire organization—which, after all, is only the extended shadow of the man who heads it. A strong negative personality who is out of tune with the ideas of the management, can extend his negative vibrations to others in an organization and do great damage, just as one rotten apple in a box will soon rot all the others.

Likewise, one woman weeping can cause others in the same room to weep. One person laughing can make others laugh. And the yawn of a single person can cause an epidemic of yawns. We seldom realize how much our emotional vibrations affect others, and how much we are affected by theirs.

If you would remain a positive type, avoid associating too much with any negative or pessimistic personalities. Many clergymen and personnel counselors often become the victims of prolonged streams of people who come to them with their troubles. The steady impact of woe and sorrow vibrations eventually reverses their positive polarity and reduces them to a negative state.

To better understand the effect of these suggestive vibrations, you need only remember your varying feelings upon entering different offices or homes. The atmosphere, the creation of the people habitually frequenting the place, can be instantly detected as upsetting, disturbing, tranquil, harmonious, cold or warm—the arrangement of the furniture, the color scheme, the very walls themselves, all vibrate to the thinking of the persons occupying the room, and bespeak what type of thoughts they think. Whether the home is a mansion or a shack, the vibrations are always a key to the personality of those who occupy it.

Are you afraid to take on responsibilities, afraid to make decisions, afraid to step out alone? Most people are—that's why there are so few leaders and so many followers. If you're confronted with a problem, the longer you put it off, the greater it becomes, and the more fearful you become of your ability to solve it. In not deciding, you fail to act, and in failing to act, you invite failure. Therefore, learn to make decisions. Experience will soon teach you that once a decision is made, problems and troubles begin to disappear. Even though your decision may not be the best one, the mere deciding gives you strength and raises your morale. It's the fear of doing the wrong thing that attracts the wrong thing. Decide and act, and chances are that your troubles will fade into thin air—whether you make a mistake or not. All great men make quick, firm decisions that flow from their intuition, their accumulated knowledge, and previous experience. So learn to be audacious in your actions.

I make no claim to being a faith-healer, but anyone who knows anything about the power of mind knows the effects of emotionalized thinking upon the condition of the body, and what suggestion can do toward bringing disease as well as curing it. Some faith-healing movements such as Christian Science effect cures by denying that the disease exists, and thousands attest to the validity of this method of healing. Followers of other schools of healing make no attempt to deny the disease, but instead ignore it, affirming that they are basically well and happy and getting better every day. Members of the various schools of thought are the best judges of the methods that work for them; but in all cases, the individual's belief determines the success of the method of cure. However, it is interesting that Christian Science, which advocates denial, has a tremendous following, and its membership continues to increase by leaps and bounds.

Just how far suggestion can cure disease and physical ailments is still a matter of great controversy among the various schools of mental healing and members of the medical profession. But many thousands in our country alone—and the number increases daily—firmly believe that a cure of their ailments came as a result of mental-healing.

It has long been known that fear, hate, and worry can lead to many bodily ills, even to fatal illnesses, although some members of the medical profession still refuse to acknowledge this. Yet as early as February 19, 1945, a *Life* Magazine article entitled "Psychosomatic Medicine," declared that during the war, 40 per cent of all Army disability cases were found to originate from psychosomatic causes. The article pointed out that many cases of hay fever, bronchial asthma, heart disease, high blood pressure, rheumatic disease, arthritis, diabetes mellitus, the common cold, and various skin conditions such as warts, hives, and allergic reactions were caused either by emotional upsets directly or by physical disturbances in which the emotions were an aggravating factor. "Psychosomatic" refers to a combination of mind and body ailments brought on by emotions; the prescribed remedy is a combination of medical treatment and psychotherapy that locates the source of the emotional disturbances and tries to eradicate it.

Because of the experiments of the psychiatrists and psychoanalysis in recent years, the whole subject of both medical and mental treatment is probably due for a complete revision, with resulting mind-cures which may prove astounding.

However, those who understand the science of psychotherapeutics are fairly well agreed that a cure does not come through the treatment of the healer nearly so much as from the patient himself. In other words, the suggestion—no matter in what form the healer gives it (whether in accordance with the principles of psychotherapeutics or in conjunction with some special religious belief)—is in turn transmitted by autosuggestion to the patient's own subconscious mind, where it becomes effective. The following statement may invite criticism, but if a patient refuses to believe in the healer's suggestive appeals, the purpose is never accomplished. The healer and the patient have to be *en rapport* to get results, and my theory is that any person who understands the use of the power of suggestion could get the same results without the aid of a healer, provided he were sufficiently strong and constant in his own convictions and suggestions. The same mirror technique, and the cards with suitable affirmations, can be used here too to great advantage.

The 1970s saw a renewed interest in telepathy or thought-transference, arising out of the experiments and investigations carried on in many colleges and universities, particularly those conducted under the direction of Dr. J. B. Rhine of Duke University. Of course, Joseph Dunninger, the self-styled mentalist of the 1950s, with his so-called feats of thought-projection and mind-reading, did much to widen popular discussion of the subject.

It has always struck me odd that many people who profess to believe in the Bible, in which there are countless stores of visions, clairvoyance, and telepathy, declare that today telepathy and kindred phenomena are not possible. The records of both the American and British Societies for Psychical Research are filled with case reports of telepathy, clairvoyance, and similar phenomena. But despite the published reports of scientific findings, many people scoff at the idea that telepathy exists.

Notwithstanding the general skepticism, some of the world's greatest scientific thinkers have declared that telepathy is not only possible but is a faculty that most people can use when they understand it. In addition to the findings of both the American and British Societies for Psychical Research and the results made public by Dr. Rhine, there are numerous books on the subject. A few of the older and better-known ones are *Mental Radio*, by Upton Sinclair; *Beyond the Senses*, by Dr. Charles Francis Potter, the well-known New York preacher; *Thoughts Through Space*, by Harold Sherman and famous explorer Sir Hubert Wilkins; *Telepathy*, by Eileen Garrett; and *Experimental Telepathy*, by René Warcollier, Director of the Institute Metaphysique International in Paris.

When the results of Dr. Rhine's experiments were first made public, many men rushed into print to declare that the results could be laid to chance. Considerable time and money were spent in an effort to prove that telepathy was non-existent. Yet the experiments continued at Duke and at other leading universities. I often wondered why many opposing so-called scientific investigators do not try to prove that the phenomena exist instead of trying to prove the contrary; but here again, I have a theory that belief is the miracle worker—and this is partly substantiated by what Dr. Rhine himself said in his book on extrasensory perception. He declared that satisfactory results were secured when the experimenters caught the "spirit of the thing"—in other words, while there was enthusiasm, spontaneous interest, and the belief that it could be done. But the ability to transmit and receive weakened once the original novelty wore off. When students were called back later to continue their experiments in the course of their studies, enthusiasm was lacking, and the results not satisfactory.

Dr. J. B. Rhine wrote an article in the August 25, 1946 *American*

Weekly magazine, captioned "Scientific Evidence Man Has a Soul." Since his explanations deal directly with the subject matter of this book, I quote the article almost in full—courtesy of the late Dr. Rhine, and with the permission of *The American Weekly.*

> *What has science to say about the soul? For the answer to this question, we would naturally turn to psychology because it is literally "the science of the soul." But here we have a surprise coming, for we find that the soul theory of man has been practically dropped from psychology books and lectures.*
>
> *Most psychologists will even smile tolerantly if one speaks of "the mind itself" as if there were such a thing apart from the brain. Everything has to be physical to be real, according to the prevailing view; anything non-physical or spiritual, as the soul is supposed to be, therefore simply has to be dismissed as pure superstition.*
>
> *However, some things occur now and then that just do not fit in at all with this physical view of man. For example, a person may awaken from a horrible dream in which a friend or relative is dying. The shocking picture turns out to be essentially true and the timing about right, although the friend may be a thousand miles away. The oddest feature of all this is that in some cases, the event perceived may not occur until hours or days after the dream; yet it may have been accurately pictured and even experienced in considerable detail.*
>
> *The first thought is, of course, that such experiences are mere coincidences. Not many people get beyond this first easy explanation, but fortunately a few have done so; and when one studies great numbers of these experiences, they lose all appearance of being accidental. The scientific thing to do, of course, was to set to work to discover what might lie behind these happenings.*
>
> *Obviously if any of these "psychic" experiences showed that the mind has the power to reach out beyond space and time, they would plainly be transcending physical law. The mind would then be demonstrated to be a spiritual rather than a physical system. Here was a clue to the soul—nothing more; but it provided the necessary lead to reliable evidence.*
>
> *From these "psychic" experiences the ESP tests were derived. ESP is the abbreviation of extrasensory perception, which includes telepathy and clairvoyance, two different modes of acquiring knowledge without the use of the recognized sense organs such as the eyes and ears. In a typical telepathy test, the person tries to identify which card or number or other symbol is being held in mind by another person—who is, let us say, located in an adjoining room. In a clairvoyance test, on the other hand, it is the object itself, commonly a card, which the percipient tries to perceive. In a word, telepathy is the ESP of the state of mind of another person; clairvoyance, the ESP of an object.*
>
> *At Duke University in 1930 a small group of psychologists began a series of ESP experiments of both types, telepathy and clairvoyance. This work was sponsored by the great British psychologist William McDougall, Fellow of the*

Royal Society, who was at the time the head of the Department of Psychology at Duke. This work, carried out in what came to be called the Parapsychology Laboratory ("para" meaning the unusual, the exceptional, the unorthodox), was by no means the first of its kind. Experiments had been done here and there, some even in universities, for as much as fifty years before. But there had been no systematic, consecutive experimentation following up the problems through the years, such as took place at Duke. That university was the first to offer a permanent haven to active research on "psychic" problems.

The Parapsychology Laboratory found fresh confirmatory evidence of both types of ESP, telepathic and clairvoyant. They developed and standardized new tests, making it easier to repeat the experiments. This had the effect of starting a movement of ESP experimentation which spread to many other institutions here and abroad. Elaborate precautions were taken to insure that no sensory cues were possible and that no error could affect the test results. The tests were of such a nature that the scores could be evaluated by standard and long-approved statistical methods. It could be shown clearly that the scores made in the tests could not reasonably be accounted for, either by chance or by experimental weakness of any kind.

Once the experimenters were satisfied that the occurrence of ESP was soundly established, they set to work on the vitally important question as to what relation that capacity had to the physical world. Do telepathy and clairvoyance operate strictly under physical law? Or do they reach beyond the limits of physics as the spontaneous "psychic" experiences seem to do?

Fortunately it was a simple matter to test ESP in relation to space. For example, we needed only to conduct tests with long distance between the cards and the person trying to identify them by ESP, and compare the results with short-distance tests. Both telepathy and clairvoyance gave as good results at great distances as they did with small. Distance measured in yards, miles, or hundreds of miles simply did not matter in the operation of ESP, as far as the experiments went. For that matter, angles, barriers, and other physical conditions seemed likewise to have no effect on success in the ESP tests.

What, then, about time? We argued that if space does not influence ESP, time should not affect it either. The tests for ESP of the future, or precognition (prophecy is a more familiar word), were easily derived from the regular ESP tests. People who could successfully identify cards extrasensorially at a distance were then asked to try to predict the order of the cards after the deck was shuffled. We found that they scored as well on decks of cards that were mechanically shuffled before checking as they did trying to identify the cards in the deck at the time. Moreover, they did as well at predicting the order of the cards ten days ahead as for a two-day period. Length of time beyond the prediction and the check-up following the shuffling made no more difference than had length of distance in the earlier experiments.

There was only one interpretation of these experiments possible—namely, that the mind of man somehow transcends the space-time limitations of the physical world. As the experiments were confirmed by other research men and women in other laboratories, the conclusion became firmly established that the mind does indeed possess properties not belonging to physics as we know it. Since space and time are the surest indications of what is physical, the mind must, therefore, be extraphysical or spiritual in nature. And all we mean by the "soul" in man is that the mind is non-physical—or spiritual—in character. The ESP experiments, then, have yielded evidence of the soul in man.

To some people this will seem a very small beginning on the problem of the soul. Certainly we must not exaggerate the extent of the findings. Actually we have done little more than produce evidence for an elemental sort of soul theory. There is, of course, a great deal more to the religious concept of the soul than has been found in these researches. There are many great problems remaining. Is the soul capable of separation from the body? Can it survive bodily death? If it can and does, can discarnate souls have any contact with the living, or in any way influence them? What about the idea of a world-soul, or God? What about communication between souls, especially the soul of man and God?

These and many other fundamental questions of religious doctrine remain untouched by anything thus far discussed in this article. All we have a right to conclude is that the physical concept of man which has increasingly prevailed in intellectual circles since the rise of materialism is now thoroughly disproved.

There is something—how much, we do not know—definitely extraphysical about humans. There is an order of reality in human life not subject to the laws of time and space.

But it is just as important, I think, to recognize, too, the tremendous possibilities we can now see. The soul-theory of man gives us much to build on in our further thinking on religious problems. We have now verified the essential foundation upon which the spiritual philosophy of man was originally erected. It remains for scientific inquiry to go on further to find out by the same methods all we can about human personality, its nature and destiny—in short, to take up the other great questions of religion.

There was a time when experimental inquiry into the problems of religion would have met with vigorous opposition from orthodox religious leaders. Many conservatives would resent the intrusion of science into the domain of what they think should be pure faith. But a great many deeply religious men and women are eagerly reaching out for a more tangible sort of knowledge regarding the human mind and all of its potentialities that lie far beyond our present knowledge.

Surprisingly enough, it has been from orthodox science that we have met the main opposition. The scientific conservative especially fears any division in nature, any such dualism as that of soul and body—so much that he is likely to refuse to look at evidence which suggests such a duality. Such anxiety is quite

> *groundless, for if, as we may now claim to know, man does have a soul as well as a body, both fundamentally different, the two are still in some sense unified. They do interact; therefore, they have something in common. Two things cannot affect each other if they differ in every single point. Therefore, there must be a world of hidden realities, probably neither physical nor mental as we know them, from which the manifestations of mind and body, the psychical and physical, originally stem. This realm beyond mind and matter lies there almost as unknown as the American continents were to Columbus, silently awaiting some fortunate explorer of the future. But he will have to be someone who, like the great Genoese sailor, was daring enough to question existing charts of knowledge and belief—and put them to experimental test.*

I have often attended séances at which the medium has refused to perform, declaring that someone in the audience was a scoffer, a nonbeliever whose vibrations were creating a hostile atmosphere. The materialistic skeptic may laugh at this, but I have attended large meetings were one lone heckler's persistent hostility has not only disrupted the audience but completely defeated the efforts of the speaker.

I think that anyone who understands the vibratory theory of thought can see why unsympathetic vibrations can be monkey wrenches thrown into the machinery. Dr. Rhine discovered in his psychokinesis tests that when a subject operated in the presence of an observer who tried to distract him and depress his scoring, the results were always below expectancy. And, contrariwise, when the same subject performed alone or in the presence of neutral or sympathetic observers, his score of successes was correspondingly high.

You have only to read the history of witchcraft, the story of voodoo medicine men and "hexers," and even the achievements of present-day mental-healers. There is undoubtedly some force at work which influences others even at a distance. The suggestion first planted in the mind of the patient (or victim, as the case may be) doesn't account for the results—especially in the absent-treatment method where the patient may have no knowledge that the healer is "working" on him. Whether telepathy is involved here is something that has not yet been established.

Practically all of the great electrical scientists, including Edison, Steinmetz, Tesla, and Marconi, were greatly interested in telepathy. Dr. Alexis Carrel not only believed in telepathy but declared that scientific men should study it, just as physiological phenomena are studied. After twenty years of investigation by its members, the secretary of the London Society for Psychical Research stated that telepathy is an actuality. Experiments at various colleges continue to pile up amazing evidence of its existence. Yet many scientific men still refuse to accept the findings. Moreover, the number of laymen carrying on investigations of their own is constantly growing, even though they are regarded in certain quarters as being eccentric and somewhat gullible. I have often wondered if those who belittle are really being fair, both to themselves and those interested in the phenomena, especially when the research work may lead to greater discoveries than hitherto dreamed possible.

Many horse and dog fanciers, especially those who have these animals as pets over a period of years, stoutly maintain the existence of telepathy between the animals and themselves. There have been countless stories of telepathic phenomena among primitive people in all parts of the world. Long years ago, a business executive told me that he got rid of people who were taking up his time by simply repeating mentally, "It's time for you to go. Leave now, Leave now." The visitor would shortly get fidgety, look at his watch or get up from his chair, and soon be on his way.

You can get the same results when visitors overstay their time in your home. When you feel it is time for them to go, simply say to yourself, "Go home now, go home now, go home now." You will find they glance around the room, looking for the clock and say, "Guess it's about time we were leaving."

Some skeptics will say that telepathy has nothing to do with this, that your facial expressions, bodily movements, signs of nervousness or weariness all warn the visitor that it is time to leave. Experiment for yourself; but take care that you give the visitor no outward sign, either by word or facial expression, that it is time to depart. You will find that at times, especially if the visitor is intent upon putting over a point or winning an argument, this procedure will not work. But the moment there is a lull in the conversation, try it, and the results will astonish you.

A number of years ago, I had my office on the second floor of a large building. Later, my firm moved up to the tenth floor. Often upon entering the elevator, I would say, "Ten, please," to the operator, and then immediately begin thinking about how I used to work on the second floor. Time after time, the elevator operator—who didn't know me or my earlier association, stopped at the second floor and then turned around to look at me.

A Pacific Coast clergyman who was a deep student of Mind Stuff told me that every time he wanted flowers in his church, he simply sent his thoughts out to members of his congregation and someone would send flowers. Every memorial window in his church, he told me, came as a result of the mental suggestions he gave whenever he felt the time was propitious for another window.

In a radio program in April, 1945, Dr. Roy Chapman Andrews told of one of the most unusual "coincidences" on record. Just after the publication of one of his songs, an American songwriter discovered that the same piece of music, note for note, had been composed and published in Germany only a short time before. That the compositions were identical to the last note makes the story more unusual than the many cases reported of widely separated people who have had the same idea at the same time. While living on the West Coast, I submitted an article to an eastern publication, only to receive a note from the editor saying he'd just accepted an article embracing the same material from another writer living in the East. Elisha Gray claimed that he had the idea of the telephone at the same time as Alexander Graham Bell. Independent simultaneous discovery often happens among writers, inventors, chemists, engineers, and composers.

Even during the preparation of this book, when suggestions were being made for changes and additions, my agent and I were often surprised to learn that we both received similar ideas at almost identical times. The idea of using the identical people as examples came to us almost simultaneously.

Early on, my publisher suggested that I expand the manuscript. I had been engaged in additional research work for a week when my adviser sent me a letter stating that he had suggested to the publisher the identical subject matter I had been working on. We found that the same thoughts had come to us at approximately the same time. Naturally, there is no way of knowing whether my adviser in New York caught my thoughts or whether I caught his—I merely report the facts.

chapter eight

Women and the science of belief

As ideas for this book occurred to me, I frequently thought of the many famous women who had used the power of belief. Once Ben Hur Lampman specifically suggested that I write about them:

"Many women may not realize they can use your science just as advantageously as men, and you should be specific in your message to them. Once they understand and apply what you give, they'll find themselves in a position to turn the world figuratively upside down. If there were some way for women of all nationalities to unite and use this science, there would be no future wars.

"Women are supreme egotists—when they get the idea they can do something, and that idea becomes thoroughly imbedded in their consciousness, they will stop at nothing to achieve their purpose. You know the old saying, 'The female of the species is more deadly than the male.' That is true, and once women understand their power—and you can give them the clue—they may actually run this whole world. 'Heaven has no rage like love to hatred turned, nor hell a fury like a woman scorned,' and once they are aroused and understand what they can accomplish, there will be no stopping them. Women are more versatile, more adaptable. Even though Napoleon declared that he made circumstances, most men are its victims, while women by their very nature of thinking make circumstances serve them."

It seems to me that today's women have the means of getting everything they set their minds to. Certainly, opportunities are all around them. In fact, never before in history was the world so open to women as it is today. Among those fields formerly restricted to men there are comparatively few in which women are not now represented. Today you'll find women in science, the fine arts, journalism, publicity, and various branches of government, all working intelligently, with full knowledge of their duties, and aware of their new opportunities and responsibilities.

When I read an article by a woman complaining that American women don't get a break, it dawned on me that if today's women don't get a break, it is the fault of no one but themselves. All they have to do is follow the examples of their sisters who have preceded them and made their own "breaks." Therefore, in the following pages I shall give examples of women who have used this science with great effectiveness.

Let us realize that women are going to play a more vital part than ever in the affairs of the world. Even before World War II, American women, although they may not be aware of it, were in a position to have things pretty much their own way, for they actually controlled the wealth of this country! Statistics showed that of the country's total wealth of approximately 300 billion dollars, about 70 per cent, or the huge sum of 210 billions, was in the possession of women.

During the war, women welders, women riveters, and the Wacs, Waves, and Spars, all had a taste of performing tasks heretofore handled only by men. To thousands of single girls and housewives who had never had an opportunity to do anything outside the home, those experiences should have pointed out opportunities for taking a more active part in the world.

As a former newspaper man, naturally I had to follow the feminist movement, and for nearly forty years I have seen the power of outstanding women. Many of the greatest reforms in America have been the ideas of women; and women were the driving force behind the ideas. Mrs. R. E. Bondurant was active in women's work, charities, the inauguration of child labor laws, the building of homes and hospitals for delinquent girls, numerous legislative measures to further the interest of women and children, and public movements to aid the blind and other handicapped people. Her nationally known record of nearly forty years was outstanding, and at seventy-one, even though a partial cripple, she was just as enthusiastic as ever and was seeking new worlds to conquer.

In her later years, Mrs. Bondurant was an ardent worker in the cause of the Chin-Uppers, an organization consisting of blind, crippled, and otherwise partly disabled men and women. In 1948, she planned to open a store where articles made by these people would be sold, with the cooperation of a number of business men. Mrs. Bondurant told me that if necessary, she was going to pay the rent out of her own pocket, but that all the profit would go to the Chin-Uppers. I spent a Sunday afternoon with her in her sitting room among her books and flowers. A pair of crutches stood in a corner near the door. (Even at her advanced age, Mrs. Bondurant got around on trolley cars, buses, and in and out of automobiles without help.) We discussed at length this matter of believing, and Mrs. Bondurant said:

> There is no question about it. I can speak from a pretty full life of seventy-one years, during which time I not only raised a family, but have taken part in various movements and activities you have long been familiar with. There is certainly something—call it power, God, or anything you wish—which is always there to sustain us in time of need. I have never seen it fail. We've just got to believe. When I look back through the years, I recall the fine women I was associated with when we were working for legislation to bring about better working conditions for women and children. It was the indomitable spirit of these women, who thoroughly believed in the righteousness of their cause, that made the legislation possible and effective.

> I am astounded that the average woman doesn't realize her tremendous power. I don't call it stupidity, because I would never admit that women are stupid. Rather, they lack interest. In talking to women's groups, I am amazed that many of them never knew that these great reform movements to help them were initiated by women. Once women become aware of their strength and power, they can do more to bring about lasting peace and make this world a better place than all the famous male warriors and would-be peacemakers.

> All the great foward movements, all the great things in this world, have been done by men and women who were dreamers and believers in their dreams coming true. They could not have accomplished things otherwise. It's like the

old story about climbing to the top of the mountain in search of that indefinable something. It makes no difference from which side the approach is made—those who steadfastly climb reach the top. So it is with this matter of believing. It isn't so much what the real or imaginary object of our belief may be, it's the belief and following through that makes the thing possible.

I don't want to appear critical, but people don't have sufficient action or driving force behind their beliefs. For example, some women's organizations will pass resolutions in favor of or against this and that, and think that settles the matter. The resolutions are no good unless the sentiments expressed are actually brought to the attention of the powers that be.

I don't know of any greater thing in life than the satisfaction that comes through serving. During the many years I spent in sponsoring various causes and getting legislation adopted, I never received a penny to cover my expenses. While it may sound like Pollyanna business to many people, bread tossed upon the waters does come back. In illustration, I might tell you that during the Depression my husband lost $80,000. He was sick in bed at home, and I would go to the office daily to get the mail and check the routine. Sometimes it looked as if we wouldn't have money to meet imperative needs, but just when we had to meet the obligations, checks would appear in the mail from people to whom Mr. Bondurant had lent money or from long-overdue accounts. We had some pretty hard times, but help always came through just in time, and I never lost my belief.

As I listened to Mrs. Bondurant, I realized that I was in the presence of no ordinary woman, but rather of a human dynamo who had the great belief, spirit, and determination to get things done. She had been credited with having had more laws in the interest of women and children passed than any other woman or organization in the state. What it would mean to the world if all women with her vision and driving force undertook to use this science?

In common with many men and women who have reached great heights, Grace Moore, she with the beautiful singing voice, won her success in the face of difficulties that would have stopped some of the strongest men. As a child, she dreamed of becoming a great opera singer. The little girl went out to win the hearts of people everywhere. Even as a penniless runaway in New York, where often she had to sing for her supper in small Greenwich Village cafés, Grace Moore never lost her courage. She made her debut at seventeen and was close to the zenith of her career at forty-five. Again and again when she appeared hopelessly defeated, she, with unquenchable courage, emerged victorious. When she lost her voice and a throat specialist told her she would never sing again, she put up a tremendous battle and emerged from a year's rest, singing more beautifully than ever.

Her glorious voice brought her great fame, and up to the time of her death in an airplane crash in Copenhagen in 1947, Grace Moore continued to believe in her dreams. She was one of the few stars who believed in helping other talented people to achieve their objectives, and her timely aid assisted many unknown aspiring singers. When one of her protégées, who had achieved success, became temperamental about her part in a performance, Miss Moore passed along another famous singer's advice: that to great artists, there was no such thing as a small part; and to small artists, there were no big parts.

Ellen Wilkinson, the fiery British Minister of Education, was a tiny, red-haired woman who drove her way upward through her persistence. Less than five feet tall, she was never cowed by the biggest of the British leaders. It is said that she made a career of annoyance, first as a school teacher, than as a suffragist, novelist, newspaper writer, and finally cabinet minister. Someone said of her that no woman in the whole of Britain had been more active, more persistent, or more annoying. She was pleased! Probably her greatest contribution was her campaign to raise the age of leaving school from fourteen to fifteen. She won this fight in the face of stiff opposition of fellow ministers and the great demand for youth in British industry.

From the time of Cleopatra, thousands of women, relying on their inmost convictions, have shaped the lives of millions. It may not be historically correct that behind every great ruler was a woman, but certainly women have had very much of a guiding hand in history-making, achieving success through their beliefs.

One was Eugenia de Montijo, who married Napoleon the Third. When a small child in Spain, she had fallen against a bannister and bruised her body. Her gypsy nurse told her not to cry, that she would be a queen and live to be a hundred. She believed in gypsies, and her fortune materialized nearly as prophesied. She became Empress Eugénia and lived until she was ninety-four, just six years less than the age fixed by her gypsy nurse.

Madame Marie Curie was the co-discoverer of radium. As a

child in Warsaw, Marja Sklodowska (later to be known as Madame Curie) was running to join a group of playmates when an old gypsy woman stopped her, demanding that the girl show her hand. The other children did not want Marja to listen to the gypsy, but the gypsy woman held on to the little hand, excitedly commenting on the remarkable lines in her palm and telling the child she would be famous.

The desire to discover what lay behind that strange phenomenon known as radioactivity, literally drove Professor Pierre Curie and his wife Marie to the epochal discovery of radium. Perhaps history will never know whether the old gypsy fortune-teller inspired Madame Curie's career. But that conclusion would appear obvious, for early in her girlhood Madame Curie made up her mind to become a scientist. She was refused permission to study science at the University of Cracow (the secretary told her that women should not concern themselves with science and suggested that she enter cookery classes). She went to Paris and entered the Sorbonne, supporting herself by teaching and working in the laboratories. There she met Pierre Curie and, once embarked with him on the task of tracking down at least one source of radioactivity, nothing stopped her. She had two daughters, a household to manage, as well as the problem of ill health, but she refused to give up laboratory work, even when her husband begged her to. Few women have been so greatly honored as Madame Curie, who certainly made those childhood prophecies come true.

Perhaps one of the strangest stories proving the great power in believing, is found in that of Opal Whiteley. This astounding historical case clearly shows that (as William James pointed out) belief creates its verification in fact; and affords unmistakable proof that often events are influenced by our very great desires. According to those who knew her in her childhood, the girl was the daughter of an American family named Whiteley, headed by an Oregon logger. She, however, believed herself to be the daughter of Henri d'Orléans, heir to the Bourbon claim to the Crown of France. She was credited with having written a diary when she was six or seven years old, which told about her "angel" father and "angel" mother of royal blood. Printed in 1920 under the auspices of the *Atlantic Monthly*, it created a sensation and precipitated a huge literary controversy that drew in psychologists, scientists, astrologers, psychics, editors, clergymen, literary critics, and almost every person who had known Opal at any time.

In Alfred Powers' *History of Oregon Literature,* there is a chapter by Elbert Bede, in which he says, "I haven't the least doubt that a large part of Opal's diary is a hoax and a large part plagiarism, and I have presented facts that show the foster parentage claim impossible." But even though Opal Whiteley may not have been born of royalty, she was actually accepted as such in later years.

The diary was printed when Opal was about twenty-two years of age. In 1933, some thirteen years after, newspapers carried a story about an American woman traveling in India. While in the state of Udaipur, she had a remarkable experience. Sitting in her carriage, she was astounded to see another carriage, coming toward her, led by a half troop of cavalry. In the other carriage was Opal Whiteley, the girl from the logging camp of Oregon. Investigators later disclosed that Opal Whiteley was actually residing in the household of the Maharaja of Udaipur, the ruling Indian prince. The same newspaper stories told how Ellery Sedgwick (editor of the *Atlantic Monthly* when her diary was printed) verified that the girl was actually residing in the royal household. They further related that Mr. Sedgwick had received substantiation of this story from the secretaries of two maharaja's courts. In his book, *The Happy Profession,* Mr. Sedgwick devotes a chapter to this strange tale.

I have had several talks with Mr. Bede (for many years a well-known Oregon newspaper man, who became editor of the *Oregon Mason)* regarding the remarkable way Opal molded her destiny. Bede said to me, "It was uncanny, almost supernatural, the way circumstances suited themselves to her plans."

Like most people who knew the girl in her childhood, Bede is absolutely convinced that Opal was born of American parents, the Whiteleys. He had known her quite well, and she had frequently been in his home in Cottage Grove. "My first knowledge of Opal came when I was reporting a Junior Christian Endeavor convention in Cottage Grove, and I was informed that a seventeen-year-old girl from a nearby logging camp had been elected president. On first impression, Opal was a vibrant, fluttery, exotic, whimsical person, informed strangely beyond her years, eager, deeply earnest, and seriously religious. She later became to me an inexplicable enigma.

"She was always planning well in advance anything she would undertake. In preparation of her nature book, *The Fairyland Around Us*, it was most amazing how she solicited contributions from such persons as Andrew Carnegie and John D. Rockefeller, and actually got money from some of them. A leaflet advertising the book carried expressions of wondering admiration from such persons as Queen Elizabeth of Belgium, Theodore Roosevelt, Nicholas Murray Butler, Gene Stratton Porter, and others of equal prominence."

I was struck by one paragraph in Mr. Bede's story: "With all these plans so well laid so long before Opal's jaunt to Massachusetts' center of culture, I have often wondered what plans she had made to give the diary to the publishers—and then how Ellery Sedgwick should accidentally ask for this diary."

Studying these words, I wondered if it really was an accident that Mr. Sedgwick asked for the diary, and whether this strange girl had not telepathically given the thought to Mr. Sedgwick. I did not discuss this point with Mr. Bede, but if Opal Whiteley knew how mentally to transmit her thoughts to others in advance, then it explains how Mr. Sedgwick "happened" to ask if she had kept a diary.

For years I have been convinced that people close to nature and those intimately associated with wild and domesticated animals have an understanding or insight that lets them see far beyond the horizons of most who live in city penthouses. I have always believed that to these people, Nature reveals many secrets withheld from those who never get nearer to a cow than a milk bottle. Is telepathy, the ability to transmit our thoughts silently so that others catch them, one of the secrets Nature reveals to those close to her? That is something I cannot answer, although it is common knowledge that primitive people in all quarters of the world have used the secret of telepathy for centuries. There are numerous books on telepathy among primitives; as a famous editor once said to me, "To accept the idea that these natives don't use it would put *us* in the class of the uninformed."

Now, let me recount what Mr. Bede had to say about Opal's

closeness to nature: "A volume would hardly suffice to summarize the personality of the nature-tutored child, who had at the age of six—as her diary would have us believe—confided her most intimate secrets to Michael Angelo Sanzio Raphael (a fir tree), and whose associates instead of people were Lars Porsena of Clusium (a crow), Thomas Chatterton Jupiter Zeus (a wood rat), Brave Horatius (a shepherd dog), Peter Paul Rubens (a pet pig), and other characters with equally classical appellations.

"In her adolescent years, Opal gathered geological specimens by the barrel, and bugs and worms by the thousands. She garnered chrysalises by the bucketful and watched how God restored life to his fairies of the great outdoors. Somewhere, somehow, she gained a prodigious amount of knowledge about these things. Without having completed a high school course, this mysterious girl presented herself at the University of Oregon, where entrance requirements were waived because of her knowledge of geology, astronomy, and biology."

According to Bede and others who knew Opal as a girl, no one ever mentioned anything that would indicate that the Whiteleys had adopted her. Bede says that only with the publication of the diary in the *Atlantic Monthly* did relatives and friends receive the first intimation that Opal claimed foster-parentage. Mr. Bede told me that what Mr. Whiteley (Opal's real or foster father) thought was that "his daughter" had been caught in the meshes of some wily promoters.

Shortly after her diary was printed, Opal Whiteley left the United States very secretly, traveling with a confidential document—not an ordinary passport—signed by our Secretary of State and Sir Edward Grey of the British Foreign Office. Just how she was able to do this amazes Mr. Bede and others who knew her in childhood. But if she was the bona fide daughter of American parents and not of Indian royal blood, we obviously have here evidences of the workings of the strange powers of the human mind, of which (I repeat!) we know little.

In 1947, Opal Whiteley was reported to be living in England. But when Mr. Bede wrote his article a number of years ago, he said, "When last definitely heard of, she had been accepted as a princess of India, through an alleged marriage of Henri d'Orléans, the 'angel' father of the diary." I asked him how Opal had been accepted as a princess of India, if she was not in fact born one. He said he couldn't explain it. Then I asked him if he thought her constant thinking so—her very deep belief—had anything to do with it.

"Frankly, I do not know. It may be, for we haven't probed to the depths of the mind and don't know the extent of its powers."

Reading Mr. Sedgwick's own story of this strange girl, he also appears convinced that Opal's real parents were the Whiteleys, and that her claim of being of royal blood was pure fantasy. But she was accepted by royalty, because Opal obviously knew a lot of secrets unknown to the average person. Here, in his own words, is Sedgwick's theory of how this child from Oregon made her vision come true:

> *I have a theory and hold to it. Among an infinity of letters came one written by an American of French parentage, whose father, he told me, was a sergeant in the Franco-Prussian War of 1870. The colonel or perhaps the general of this sergeant's division was Prince Henry of Bourbon. Toward the close of his life the Prince, traveling across America, stopped in Oregon to chat with his old soldier. Whether or not this is fact, I cannot say, but my correspondent had no doubt of it: first among his childhood memories, was the prince's arrival at his father's cottage door. "I sat on his knee," he told me, and I believed him.*

> *Now, according to my theory, the visit of a Prince of the Blood to an Oregon hamlet was an event. The truth and the legend of it spread through the lumber camps. What is more likely than that such a tale captivated the mind of a lonely and imaginative child, and that her daydreams centered about it? At the heart of every little girl, Cinderella sits enthroned. With Opal, the legend grew to be true.*

> *The truth magnified with the years, and finally permeated her entire mind, her fancy, and her life.*

> *Such is my theory of Opal's childhood. In after years, the story becomes an attested record of fact and yet, to my thinking, loses nothing of its wonder thereby. Opal, who had come to be petted and patronized by many notable people in New York and Washington, grew sick of it all. She went to England, always making friends, took up the faith of her "father," and established herself in a Catholic community at Oxford.*

> *Then one day I had startling news of her. A friend of my youth, Mrs. Rosina Emmet Sherwood, wrote me asking if it was possible to believe a correspondent of hers who stated that she had seen Opal sitting like the princess in the story in an open barouche driving in state down the streets of Allahabad, royal outriders clearing the way for H.R.H. Mlle. Françoise de Bourbon!*

> *The story was credible, for it was true—I verified it beyond conjecture! First I wrote to Opal, who sent me a collection of photographs of her Indian tour.*

There she was, perched in a howdah on an elephant's back, ready for a tiger hunt. (Henri de Bourbon was famous for his bag of thirty-six tigers, and I recalled Opal chanting French verses in honor of his victory). There she stood, the center of many another turbaned group.

Photographs can be liars, and many of them stem from Hollywood, which hardly contradicts the term. I was not satisfied. Since Opal's narrative claimed that two of the greatest maharajas had been her hosts, I wrote to both their courts. In due time two letters, emblazoned with regal crests, each informed me the writer's royal master bade the secretary reply that it had been his high privilege to entertain H.R.H. Mlle. Françoise de Bourbon, and that a series of fêtes had been given in her honor.

The wonder of all this had not subsided when an unsolicited letter arrived from a lieutenant colonel of His Majesty's forces occupied with maneuvers at Aldershot, informing me with some asperity that the colonel himself had been honored by an order to attend an official garden party given for Her Royal Highness' entertainment. Further, he begged to ask who had questioned the authenticity of the lady who had graced the occasion.

"I close this account on a melancholy note. In the journal Opal sent to accompany her photographs, no vestige remained of the contagious fascination of an earlier day. She described things as they are. The dew of the morning had vanished. The hard sunlight of middle age beat down upon a world that everybody sees only too clearly. The fairy kingdom was now the playground of other children. Its gates were closed, and Opal stood outside.

But while she was still the Opal of the Journal of an Understanding Heart, *she had had her vision, and the vision was true. No truth is more certain than that which brightens the heart of childhood."**

Some readers may question this weird story, but those are the facts. Obviously, as Sedgwick states, "The child who wrote Opal's diary believed in it. She knew it for her own."

From early Biblical times, there have been prophets, oracles, soothsayers, astrologers, and fortune-tellers. As a hard-boiled newspaper man, I have investigated a number of so-called seers. While some were obviously charlatans of the first water, others mystified me. Certainly many of these fortune-tellers believe in their ability to foretell the future. Materialists will say that that is impossible. Having spent years in research work, I am not so positive, for some of the great prophecies of the past have actually been fulfilled.

Even though many deride the ability of astrologers, fortune-tellers, and the like, millions of people in this world believe in prophecies, including some of our greatest financiers, statesmen, actors and actresses, and people in all walks of life. No matter what my views about the ability of anyone to foretell the future, I have long thought that it wasn't so much what the prophets foretold as it was the subjects' reliance on what the soothsayer predicted for them that brought certain things to pass. In other words, the seer planted a suggestion in the form of a prophecy in the individual's subconscious mind, which immediately went to work to make it come true. I believe that in the cases I have cited, the power of suggestion, working in the individual to make the prophecy a reality, finally produced the outcome.

Marie Dressler, the silent screen actress, probably evoked more laughter than any other actress of her time. Those who saw her in *Tillie's Nightmare*, and *Tugboat Annie*, will never forget that great personality. But Marie Dressler had a very hard time, suffering many privations before she became a screen star known to millions. Whether true or not, I have heard that the advice and prediction of astrologers landed Marie Dressler at the top.

In this connection, I had a strange experience shortly before Miss Dressler's death. In explanation, I firmly believe that when people get on a certain plane of thinking or are attuned with their subconscious minds, they automatically become *en rapport* with one another. Shortly after I had written my book, *T.N.T.—It Rocks the Earth*, it hit me in a flash that all great men and women had been using what I had outlined. I set out to verify this by writing outstanding men and women for their views and comments.

Marie Dressler was one of the first women I selected, probably because I was her ardent admirer. I heard her on the radio one night and knew instantly that she had a grip on that "something" which many people seek and seldom find. It is common knowledge that very few great screen stars personally acknowledge letters from unknowns. But I knew if I wrote Miss Dressler, I would get a reply. When I dictated the letter, my secretary volunteered that Marie Dressler would never acknowledge it. We even made a small wager, as I did later with several others.

While I felt that Miss Dressler would respond immediately, I was astounded at the sight of her enclosure—a check for twenty copies of my brochure. In her letter she said:

"Thank you so much. Oh! what a book, if used rightly. As I read through it—and look back, which I very seldom do, and check up on my own life—it looks as though I had been going down the right path."

Now that this great woman is long dead, her letter is among my cherished possessions. I never had personal correspondence with a woman who had put so much heart and soul into her work to cheer up humanity, yet who had had more personal trouble or who had put up a greater fight to reach the pinnacle of success.

Incidentally, there are two fine thoughts in her letter. First, it is futile to dwell on the past. It is apparent Miss Dressler discovered this a number of years before her death, realizing that she couldn't give full thought to future accomplishments if she cluttered up her mind with thoughts of the past.

Second, as she indicated in ordering extra copies of my brochure, she was always trying to help people. That may be a forlorn gesture in many instances; but she must have realized that extending such help brings its own reward.

Helen Keller was a marvel to me. As the world knows, she was deprived of her sight, hearing, and speech when she was twenty months old. Yet through her talks and her many articles and books, she became an inspiration to thousands less handicapped than she. When Helen Keller, through stupendous effort, learned to speak, she gave to the world a new vision of what the handicapped could do once they believed in their ability to achieve.

It is interesting that Helen Keller was a confirmed Swedenborgian. As many readers may know, Swedenborg lived in the early days of the eighteenth century and was a very unusual man, perhaps one of the world's greatest mystics. He too, could foresee the future, anticipating the submarine, the machine gun, flying machines, and the horseless carriage that would go twenty miles an hour. I don't know whether Swedenborg could be called a spiritualist, but he certainly had something far beyond the ken of the average person. He believed greatly in the power of the mind and had trances, visions, and strange dreams which must have come via his subconscious.

Another outstanding woman was the subject of much controversy (and her name is known to millions because a motion picture depicting her life was shown throughout the world). In 1940, Sister Elizabeth Kenny brought from Australia an idea for treating polio victims. As a nurse, she had discovered what is known as the "hot pack system," a method of applying hot-water packs to the afflicted portions of the victim's body. Although she was ridiculed by many people professional and unprofessional, Sister Kenny persistently, forcefully brought her principles of treatment to the American public's attention and through her efforts established the Sister Kenny Institute at Minneapolis.

One has only to study a photograph of Sister Kenny's rugged features to see the reflection of a powerful mind, which—aided by a ready tongue—ultimately help her force her way to victory. In her native Australia she was fought at every turn, and only through the woman's sheer persistence did the American medical profession finally give her recognition.

Few women have been the subject of more controversy. From what one reads about Sister Kenny, she was convinced to the *nth* degree that her methods were right and practicable. Even though the world might attempt to discredit her, she could go marching bravely on. Here is an example of a woman with an idea, a single-ness of purpose, and the utmost belief in the efficacy of her methods of treatment who brought new hope for many polio sufferers.

The dynamic power in some women can continue into their later years. Captain Mary Converse's exploits were given in newspaper articles early in 1947. Mrs. Converse at seventy-five, a veteran of nearly 34,000 seafaring miles, wanted to go to sea again. Born in Boston, she learned seafaring from her late husband, Harry E. Converse, owner of a steam yacht. As a junior navigator, she sailed the seven seas, obtained her second pilot's license in 1935 and her captain's license in 1940. Approximately 2,600 navy officers learned navigation from Mrs. Converse. She taught them in the dining room of her Denver home!

Who's Who lists biographical sketches of outstanding women in business and the professions, including a number of executives making more than $150,000 a year. But our history recognizes no greater business woman than Lydia E. Pinkham. Her name may not be so well known today as in 1900, but the business she established and its product, Lydia Pinkham's Vegetable Compound, became household words. From a single idea, she built a huge business that brought a return of millions.

I know nothing about the efficacy of Mrs. Pinkham's Vegetable Compound, but as a boy I can remember often seeing a bottle of it in the family medicine chest. Mrs. Pinkham and her business associates really modernized advertising, for she was one of the greatest of all advertisers. Ideas used in many later advertisements were originally voiced by Mrs. Pinkham. With much of her advertising she tied in a sort of homely philosophy embodying emotional appeals to women, which resulted in millions of dollars in sales of her vegetable compound and brought tons of enthusiastic testimonials to her laboratory at Lynn, Massachusetts.

Once more, this remarkable woman demonstrated what belief in personal achievement can accomplish. During Lydia Pinkham's early life, many people were interested in the manufacture of home remedies, and she, too, started making her compound in her kitchen. For some time, she gave the mixture away to ailing women neighbors, only to realize later that it could be sold. Then she began promoting it. Like most people who start with a new idea, she had many discouragements—lack of finances, the opposition of others, and manufacturing and sales difficulties. But nothing daunted this New England woman. Her tremendous driving force and enthusiasm reached and engulfed every member of her family— especially after her business really got going!

No book documenting the great power of believing would be complete without mention of Mrs. Mary Baker Eddy, another New England woman who built up that huge religious organization known as Christian Science. As almost everyone knows, Mrs. Eddy was faced with discouragement, strife, and the bitterest ridicule. But after she gave to the world her *Science and Health with Key to the Scriptures*, based on the writings of Phineas T. Quimby, she began to develop powerful leadership, a tremendous and unshaken belief in her teachings, and a dynamic personality which has left its imprint upon millions throughout the world. Few writings have done so much to influence the sciences of medicine and theology as hers. Christian Science is another practical demonstration of the power of believing.

The world will always be indebted to Florence Nightingale, who was greatly instrumental in saving the lives of thousands and brought the nursing profession to the high standard now recognized by the entire world. Here again is a woman who knew early in life what she wanted and who set out to realize her ambition. She came from one of the richest families in England, but was born with a passion to nurse the wounded and the sick. At the time she undertook her great work, nursing was not even recognized as a profession. She started in by scrubbing the corridor floor at the Fliedner Nursing School in Germany. She soon showed that she could not only scrub floors but bind wounds, and revive patients' hopes with her encouraging talk. She, too, was fought at every turn, but being inspired with the vision of the destiny which she thought was hers, obstacles meant nothing to her. She hated bigots, believing that all should be cared for, regardless of faith, color, or creed, and she had a quick tongue when aroused.

During the Crimean War, the British War Office scoffed that Florence Nightingale's work would only result in failure. Reluctantly they let the "madcap" have her own way. At her own expense, she organized a private expedition of nurses and took them to Scutari. Even though the officers in charge of the hospital there wanted no woman to interfere with their work, interfere she did. Under her leadership, the women took over the handling of the hospital. Throughout her stay in the Crimea, her iron will constantly fought against a stone wall of opposition. Some of the most powerful statesmen of Great Britain ridiculed this astonishing woman's work and did everything possible to stop her reforms. But her letters, "filled with dynamite," awakened her countrymen until she was adored everywhere. Something had to give way, and this time it was the stone wall.

When, at the age of eighty-two, she became sick, her nurse tucked her into bed, only to have Florence Nightingale get out of her own bed and tuck in her nurse. At the age of ninety, just before she died, a friend asked her if she knew where she was. She replied, "I am watching at the altar of murdered men and I shall be fighting their cause."

When we think of martyrs, most people have in mind men who have died or been jailed for espousing causes in which they believed. Let us remember that many outstanding women of history have suffered martyrdom as much as men, from Joan of Arc who was burned at the stake to women of modern times who were jailed because of their efforts in furthering civil rights and protesting nuclear proliferation.

The name of Carrie Nation is probably fading in the memory of many, but during the years around the turn of the century, she was one of the greatest of women martyrs. Convinced that she was "divinely" appointed to destroy the saloons, Carrie Nation set out to end the illegal sale of liquor in her own state of Kansas. Aided by some of her followers, Mrs. Nation succeeded in closing many illicit barrooms by public prayer and denunciation. When she saw this method was slow in its effectiveness, she took to wielding a hatchet, smashing bottles and beer kegs and demolishing bar fixtures. She was constantly ridiculed and frequently jailed, but so thoroughly was she convinced of the righteousness of her cause that she gladly accepted her sentences.

The legendary actress Sarah Bernhardt had the temper of a tigress, yet history records her as one of the greatest emotional actresses of all times. She suffered innumerable failures in her early days on the stage, but she had a passion to make good, and by the time she was twenty-four she was famous. A woman who smoked cigars and drank strong drinks, she was a creature of extraordinary moods. An individualist in the highest sense, she would visit cemeteries and sit on tombstones as if in grief for the departed and later took to sleeping in a coffin. Sarah Bernhardt never appeared concerned with what people thought about her, though as a matter of fact, she reveled in their comment. Even though she had to wear an artificial leg toward the end of her life, she continued her stage work, for nothing could change her lifelong belief that she was a supremely great dramatic actress—and she was to the end of her life in 1923.

The dynamic Madame Schumann-Heink was an exemplification of what belief can do, once the mind gets into action. She was inspired early in life, giving to the world her beautiful voice when she became an opera singer at the age of fifteen. She too became famous in the Old World, but when she came to America, it was the fulfillment of a dream that had burned within her for many years. Her heart was torn many times, but even in the face of overwhelming odds, Madame Schumann-Heink always came smiling through. Here was a woman whose oldest son had gone off in World War I to fight for the Kaiser, while her other four boys were in the opposite trenches. But among those who heard her sing "The Star-Spangled Banner" in her quaint, foreign accent, many took off their hats and wept. Over a national radio hookup, her voice became known to millions. She was beloved by everyone and she had that basic thing—born in most people but seldom aroused—the spirit of never quitting. It was at the age of seventy-two, when she was signed up as a successor to Marie Dressler, that the curtain rang down on this great performer.

Who has heard Marian Anderson's wonderful contralto voice without being charmed and deeply moved? Yet few realize this great artist's very humble background. As a child of six she wanted a violin; at the time, she could earn five or ten cents by scrubbing doorsteps in Philadelphia. If ever a woman believed in her dreams and made them come true, it was Marian Anderson; she climbed to world fame and yet had to overcome—especially in our country—many handicaps and prejudices. Her triumph is one of the most dramatic in musical history. In Washington, D.C., on Easter Sunday 1939, this black woman of humble origin, standing before the Lincoln Memorial, thrilled an audience of 75,000 people studded with cabinet members, senators, congressmen, and famous people in business and society. I am convinced that Marian Anderson, too, succeeded through her belief, and that the great source of her inspiration came from her subconscious mind.

Let me introduce here a well-known woman who tells how her subconscious mind was directly responsible for her success. Angela Lansbury, the Tony Award-winning actress of stage and screen, was interviewed by Mildred Mesirow for *Reach Magazine*. The interviewer tells us:

The brilliant young screen star, aside from having beauty and dramatic ability, Angela Lansbury, was also a girl with an exceptionally good brain.

During a rest interval here [Hollywood] she launched forth upon one of her favorite themes—her faith in her own destiny . . .

"Ah," she amended quickly, "I think perhaps I've phrased that badly. I don't mean anything magical or occult. Perhaps faith in the power of the subconscious mind would be a better way of saying it."

"In the manner of Tennyson, perhaps, or Stevenson?" I suggested.

"Exactly! Not that I think my abilities in any way resemble their genius, you understand. But I think I've learned how to tap the resources of the subconscious. Everyone knows that the subconscious mind stores all sorts of abilities, memories, and aptitudes we don't ordinarily utilize . . . What I'm trying to say is that, when you've learned how to draw on your subconscious powers, there's really no limit to what you can accomplish."

Angela has schooled herself in the technique of this self-suggestion. Since she first chose acting as a career, she had constantly held in her mind a picture of what she aspires to achieve. From time to time she has even written down the goals she wants to reach. Obviously, she has tapped the reservoirs of creative material which few of us know how to use. Within the subconscious lie the materials of genius itself; of powers which, when properly recognized, may burst into the mental field of activity in patterns which surpass our conscious abilities . . .

"And how do you go about tapping your subconscious mind?" I asked.

"Heavens! I don't want to sound stuffy and highbrow, but it's really awfully simple. If you tell yourself over and over again that there's no limit to the creative power within you, that's about all there is to it. Honestly, I believe that's true. Whatever intelligence or creative force, or whatever it is, that resides in the world is like . . ." she waved a strong, beautiful hand expressively . . . "oh, like light or air, or something of that sort. It doesn't belong to me, especially. It's there, to be tapped and expressed by anyone who knows how to get at it.

"This isn't a cut-and-dried formula for success by any means," she continued. "It doesn't let you off hard work. You've got to keep plugging like mad, perfecting whatever kind of expression you've got; adding constantly to your skill, whether it's in acting or painting, or even making a dress. So that, when the chance for self-expression does come, when the time arrives for you to call on your subconscious power to express itself, you have a good set of tools for it to work with; a proper medium through which your creative urge can be portrayed . . . Catch on?" she added with typical humor.

"About the suggestibility of the subconscious?" I prompted.

"Oh that! Well, when you're about to drop off to sleep, just tell yourself that tomorrow's the day you've got to surpass anything you did today. That, *whatever demands are made upon you, all your abilities, all you've learned, perhaps things you've forgotten you ever knew—all these will be available to you . . .*

"Bearing in mind an actual mental picture of the situation is even better. If you're scheduled to do a screen test, for example, you see yourself acting out that test better than anyone's ever done it before. Act it like mad in your mind! Be Duse; be Bernhardt! In your mental picture, be the best there is! And when the actual test comes off, you find, often to your surprise, that you're acting better than you know how.

"The subconscious is a pretty dramatic factor in personality, I believe. It likes to act and sing and paint and express itself. It likes to surpass in anything it's called on to do. Your responsibility is to equip it with tools for expression, to give it a chance, and then make it an ally behind the scenes . . ."

Many famous women, including the Brontë sisters, Elizabeth Browning, Susan B. Anthony, Evangeline Booth, Jane Addams, attained niches in the hall of fame. *Uncle Tom's Cabin,* which many claim brought on the War Between the States, was written by Harriet Beecher Stowe, a wisp of a woman whose name will be remembered as long as there is American history. In 1850 Mrs. Stowe swore a solemn oath that she would write something "that would make the whole nation feel what an accursed thing slavery is." For two months she tried in vain to think of a story. In February, 1851, while she was attending communion service at the college church, there came to her mind the picture of Uncle Tom and of his death. Mrs. Stowe went home in tears and when she had written out the scene of Uncle Tom's death and read it to her family, they, too, were weeping.

She did a great deal of research in trying to secure factual material, but when she actually sat down to write, she needed none of it. The story obsessed her and literally wrote itself. Out of her subconscious mind surged long-forgotten memories and photographic impressions, arranging themselves almost automatically in proper sequence on paper. Mrs. Stowe didn't think out these incidents and their background, she actually saw them. To her dying day, Mrs. Stowe insisted that God, and not she, had written this book. While little was known of the subconscious mind in her time it is obvious that it was the source of this novel.

While it is too early to tell the complete story, there are three women whose names will probably go down in history as having shaped the destinies of millions of Chinese. These are the famous Soong sisters, perhaps the best known of whom is Madame Chiang Kai-shek; the others married respectively Dr. H. H. Kung and Dr. Sun Yat-sen, both Chinese leaders.

As we come down to the present day, we run across such people as Mrs. Matthew Astor Wilks, one of the richest women in the world and the daughter of the late Hetty Green who herself amassed a fortune of over $67,000,000. Mrs. Wilks followed in the footsteps of her famous mother.

The account of Vera Nyman is literally another story of rags to riches. An idea, fifteen dollars, and a bathtub put her into a business for which Mrs. Nyman once refused a million dollars. When she married her husband, Bernard, in 1920, she had the belief that she and her husband were going to make a million dollars. Mrs. Nyman rang doorbells selling a liquid cleaner and later, by cooking chemical stews night after night in her own home, hit upon a combination of ingredients that would clean 90 per cent of painted surfaces. Her product became known to millions of housewives and in 1947 alone, her sales topped $2,500,000. Mrs. Nyman, who day after day of making personal calls encountered more than 50,000 housewives, knew what it meant to face discouragement. But her belief that she would ultimately make a million dollars never faltered. It took her twenty-seven years to achieve her objective, but she had it within her grasp when a drug concern offered her $1,000,000 for her plant.

Success stories embrace dozens of women, such as Mary Dillon, president of the Brooklyn Borough Gas Company, who started in as a six-dollar-a-week office helper in the $5,000,000 corporation which she came to head. Before World War I, Mrs. Ora H. Snyder of Chicago, with a capital of only five cents, began building up a candy business centered around several shops and which was, at one time, worth more than a million dollars.

For a number of years Bertha Brainard was program director of the National Broadcasting System. With a salary that ran into five figures; she was said to be one of the highest paid women radio executives. It all came about through her getting an idea for feature radio programs. That was in 1922 and her first effort brought her a return of $50. Indeed, an entire book could be written about women who have achieved fame and fortune in the field of radio and motion pictures as artists, writers, and executives. The name of Barbra Streisand is known to millions, not only as a screen favorite but also as a motion picture director.

The whole world knows the story of Amelia Earhart, famous American aviatrix who was lost with her plane in the South Pacific. While a teacher and a social worker, she became interested in aviation and became the first woman to cross the Atlantic in an airplane. In 1931, she made a solo flight across the Atlantic and four years later flew the Pacific alone from Honolulu to California.

One writer has said that the vast majority of American men do not believe that women are even their equals. But when we stop to examine the record, the list of women who have achieved success in every line of endeavor is an impressive one. Now, since the Women's Liberation movement, there are thousands of outstanding women—from great educators to bankers and industrialists, to say nothing of the numerous writers, editors, and other professionals.

Here is the story of a woman who scored a double success—as a homemaker and a career woman. She is Mary Roberts Rinehart, who thrilled mystery fans for more than fifty years. Necessity forced her to make some money to retrieve the family fortunes which she and her doctor-husband had lost in a stock-market crash. With one hand, she wrote those great works of fiction which gained her more than ten million readers, while with the other hand, she tended her children and handled the details of housekeeping.

Many women remain single simply because they feel deeply about their careers and are not willing to marry any man who is not supportive. But surely if this science of creative thinking can work for men, it can work also for women—even to the point of woman's actually creating an image of the man of her desires and literally bringing him into reality. In other words, if a "liberated" woman visualizes the kind of man she wants and steadfastly holds to the thought, in accordance with the principles of this science, she can bring into her presence the object of her mental picture.

This may sound silly to some readers, but I have given this science to many women who have used it most effectively. Therefore, if you want a certain type of man to walk into your life, merely picture him—not necessarily in physical form but in the abstract, setting forth in your thought projection the attributes that you would like your man to have. The day will surely come when you will meet him.

In a way, it is perhaps superfluous for me to call women's attention to the advantage of using their subconscious mind, for they have always used it. As a matter of fact, they are experts in its use—only they have always thought of it as woman's intuition. My point is that the subconscious is much more than intuition. It possesses great forces which can be set in motion for the benefit of men and women through the application of the power of dynamic believing. As I pointed out earlier, wonderful results are brought about by the conscious mind's conveying the will-to-do through believing to the subconscious. This immediately sets the subconscious in action to carry out the individual's desires.

Now the women of modern times have a unique twofold mental advantage. The skilled use of their subconscious mind, characteristic of their sex, has been highly developed and has been their unconscious, though intuitive, guide through the ages. In addition, their conscious minds have been specially developed by the scientific method of modern education. I think this combination accounts for the speed with which women have acquired proficiency in so many of the so-called masculine subjects; for women's emerging from the traditional life within the home. As they enter into the world, their view of people and practical affairs is broadened and made more objective. Even women in the home have a better comprehension of how men work as well as a deeper interest in their children's future careers.

My fundamental aim is to show how each person can develop his or her plus-powers, the seeds of which lie within his subconscious mind. These plus-powers will enable you to obtain the things you want and become what you would like to be—in addition to what you have and are already. By this new co-operation of the conscious and subconscious minds, you can gain things deeply necessary to your life and happiness, and also keep undergoing personal development, no matter how long you live.

Always remember that the subconscious mind, besides being the seat of intuition, is a repository of great power and inexhaustible resources. The more you call upon these resources, the more are placed at your disposal. Remember also: the subconscious is ageless. It can never grow old or tired, and you can draw upon it all your life. The only thing you need is the power of believing—sincerely, strongly, and completely. Once the subconscious receives your message and understands your desires and ambitions, it will be only a short time before your desire will be fulfilled and your ambition achieved.

I want to impress upon my women readers that they have the same two minds, conscious and subconscious, and that through co-operation of the two minds, they can use this science and succeed just as men have. It is all a matter of believing, according to the principles here set forth. The magic that comes from believing is real, for it has been demonstrated in the lives of some of the most successful. It can be demonstrated in your life—by your own personal believing.

chapter nine

Belief makes things happen

In 1944 a popular magazine ran a story about a group of scientists in Chicago who were experimenting with moths. A female moth of rare species was placed in a room, and a male moth of the same species was released four miles away. In a few hours, the male moth was found beating its wings against the window of the room in which the female was confined. The editor declared that he believed that ideas fly—with the sureness with which the female moth communicated her whereabouts to the male—across incredible barriers to the one mind for which they are originally intended.

Here is a simple experiment that will make you wonder whether the birds don't possess telepathic or clairvoyant power. Put some scraps of bread in the backyard. There isn't a bird in sight. But hardly have you entered the house before birds begin to congregate. First come sparrows then wrens. In two or three minutes, the yard is filled with birds. Put out anything but food, and not a bird appears. What brings them to your yard? How do they know the bread is food for them? Science can give no answers.

In his broadcast of February 17, 1947, Edwin C. Hill stated that the more scientists investigate, the more they are convinced that birds and insects have a wireless of their own or some other invisible manner of communication with one another. This theory has long been expounded by nature students, and many books have been written on the subject, notably one by William J. Long, *How Animals Talk.*

During World War II, the Army Signal Corps experimented with carrier pigeons and short-wave radio. They found that the pigeons were affected by the radio waves and often, when confused, flew in circles and were lost. Consider that the swallows of San Juan Capistrano, California, fly away each October 23 and return each March 19 with unfailing punctuality. Tagged salmon released from Columbia River points spend four years in the Pacific Ocean, then consistently return to the spots from which they departed. Cats and dogs taken many miles from their homes have returned. Wild ducks and geese wing their way back to their original localities. Are we not faced with the fact that telepathic forces operate in the fish, bird, and animal kingdoms, in fact, in everything around us?

Some writers claim that all living things have the means of communicating with each other, and this may not be so farfetched after all. Early in 1945, radio listeners heard the voices of blinded soldiers telling of their experiences in "Facial sight," through which they were able to detect objects in their paths through a sixth sense or kind of "mental radar." Dr. Jacob Levine, a Boston psychologist, had charge of the school at Old Farms, in the Avon district of Connecticut where warblinded veterans were taught the use of this sixth sense. He declared that he could not explain its mechanics, but he knew that it worked. This "Facial sight" is based on the hypothesis that the body radiates definite rays of an unknown variety which, coming into contact with an object, assemble or group themselves in such form as to make a picture of it, after which they return, still bearing the picture, to the blinded person, who "sees" the returning rays as they radiate through his body.

I have long been convinced that various forms of telepathy or thought-transmission are used every day of our lives, far more than most people suspect. I believe that many leaders, preachers, orators, executives, and so-called super-salesmen, exercise the power to varying degrees, some unconsciously and others thoroughly conscious of its workings. We meet a person, and before a word is spoken, we experience a like or dislike. What causes the feeling to register but some form of thought-transmission? I have already stated that the only possible explanation of healing and affecting others at a distance is through the medium of this phenomenon, of which we are only now beginning to get a scientific explanation.

I have often sat in a famous lawyer's office as he dictated letters concerning business affairs. When he dictated, he always paced the floor, and his concentration was intense. Once I asked him why he stood while dictating—and how it happened that his letters always accomplished the end intended.

"In the first place," he replied, "I think better on my feet. Before I start dictating and during the whole period that I talk, I visualize before me the person to whom I write the letter. If I do not know him, I try to picture him as I think he may look. In both cases, I direct all my words to him in person, as though he were actually before me in the flesh and tell him mentally that my premises are right and that he should follow them."

A successful book saleswoman told me that if a customer really wanted to purchase a book, but was hesitating between two choices, she would keep repeating to herself—but directing her thought to the customer—the title of the one best suited to him. She added that many of her sales were made by thought-directive power. An automobile executive told me that when he had a prospect, he always said to himself, "You're going to buy this car, you're going to buy this car"—and the prospect did.

Very few people like to believe they are influenced by the silent thoughts of others when it comes to a matter of doing anything. But the fact remains that this invisible power exists, and all of us are subject to this subtle influence, be it telepathy or anything else you want to call it. A little experimenting on your part will convince you that it is both formidable and active.

I am certain that mothers unknowingly use it on their children, and often children use it on their parents. Not infrequently husbands and wives use it on one another, especially where a man and wife are closely attuned to one another. You who are married and have never used this science have a new field to explore!

One of the most striking examples of this subtle influence in action came to my attention several years ago. The president of a company I had been helping was dissatisfied with his sales manager, but because of the man's many years of service he didn't wish to discharge him. "I was at my wits' end," he told me, "when I suddenly got the idea that I could suggest to him mentally that he ought to resign and become a salesman instead of remaining as manager. I thought about it for hours one night. The first thing next morning, he came into my office, saying that he would like to resign as manager, since he felt that he could make more money by getting out on the street as a salesman.

"I nearly fell off my chair. I don't know whether I was guilty of using some sort of magic. But my conscience is clear, because the man today is making twice as much money as he did as sales manager. He's much happier, and we're all going to town."

A husband and wife once came to see me. The man told me that until a few months before our meeting, he had been one of the largest clothing manufacturers in the Midwest, but had sold out and was now traveling the country. "For more than thirty years," he said, "I had been a member of one of the largest and oldest secret organizations in the world which embraces this theme of believing from A to Izzard. But I, like thousands of others, never had my mind opened to it and I never realized the 'truths' contained therein. However, several years ago I attended a series of lectures on the subject of mind control, and for the first time my eyes were opened to what a wonderful power man could make available for himself. I could see how it would work in our business to tremendous advantage, and I used it. Needless to say, our business started to increase as soon as I put it to work, and it has been increasing ever since. During the Depression, when firms like ours were having a terrific struggle, we consistently made money, and when I sold out my interests, I can say with all modesty that I was at the top."

At this point his wife entered the conversation: "Before he started, my husband wouldn't openly scoff at me when I talked about this subject and what I had learned at the lectures. But he believed I was wasting my time. I just knew there was something to it, and I was certain that if my husband could get hold of it, it would mean a great deal more business for him. I talked and talked to him about attending the lectures, and then one day I realized I was doing the wrong thing. Instead of talking to him, I should use the very science I had been taught. I went at it with a vengeance. Several times a day, both my daughter and I kept repeating to ourselves mentally, 'Dad is going to go, Dad is going to go.' It took us nearly three weeks, but Dad did go."

Here the husband broke in: "You speak about your tap-tap idea. Well, she certainly worked it on me. When she first talked about what she had heard at the lectures, I just couldn't believe them to be true. I had been brought up in a very practical business world, and couldn't get myself to believe in many of the so-called abstract things. However, one day 'something' impelled me to go with her. I didn't know at the time that the 'something' was my wife's mental suggestion, and I had no idea that she and my daughter had been working on me. However, it was the greatest thing that ever happened to me. After the first lecture, I did some experimenting, and our business began to improve—and continued to improve until the day I sold out.

"Don't get me wrong. I am not religious in an orthodox sense, and what I talk about is not goody-goody stuff, but an exact science. What we think or contemplate develops into reality. We radiate our thoughts, perhaps unconsciously, to others, and we affect them. We give forth vibrations of dislike or hatred which we engender in ourselves—and, bingo, they come right back and floor us. All one needs to do is to study and understand the law of cause and effect, and it all becomes plain.

"Thought has been referred to as a powerful unseen influence, and so it is. There are so few people you can talk with on this. Most people ignorant of the subject look at you askance when you mention something about it, and now I understand why Jesus spoke in parables. However, it probably won't be many years before people generally are into the subject up to their ears. Thousands of enlightened people are recognizing that we are on the threshold of great developments in thought power, and the number is rapidly increasing. I wonder why more men don't catch hold of it and apply it in their businesses, but I guess most are like I used to be—they keep their minds closed, and no one ever takes the trouble to work on them as my wife did on me. All a person has to do is to believe, earnestly and sincerely, that such a power of mind exists and then conscientiously apply the science. It's all just as you say: when one starts tapping the subconscious mind—your own or others—the bricks fall into place as though by magic. Does it work? And how!" Alfred F. Parker, a highly respected general insurance agent in the Pacific Northwest, wrote to me in 1937, in connection with the use of this science. I do not know whether Mr. Parker was even interested in the subject of telepathy, but he thoroughly believed in the efficacy of belief. His letter speaks for itself:

> *Recently I had an opportunity to put into further practice your tap-tap idea, and I thought that you might be interested in knowing the circumstances. I have a small son who on December 29, 1936, picked up some obscure infection. For days he lay desperately ill in the hospital. There was grave doubt that he would live. I was in terrible anguish, but I resolved to meet the situation as best I could. Taking a tip from you, I put his picture on my desk and carried another in my pocket. Every hour of the day I looked at them and repeated to myself, "He will recover. He will recover."*
>
> *At first I felt I was lying to myself, as he hardly seemed to have an even chance. However, I kept it up and gradually found myself believing what I kept repeating. At just about that time, thanks to the best medical and nursing attention and some of a friend's blood transfused to him, the boy actually did begin to recover. He is now at home and regaining his strength fast.*
>
> *It may have been mere coincidence that the time when empty words began to turn into belief was the time when recovery began. But at least such coincidence is worthy of note.*

Some people have walked into a darkened room and felt the presence of someone there, even before a word was uttered. Certainly, nothing but the vibrations of some unseen individual could have indicated his presence to the other person. Evidence of telepathy? What do *you* think? It is maintained that if, at the entry of the second person, the first person in the room thinks of something entirely foreign to himself and dismisses all thought of the possibility of his discovery, the second person will not sense his presence. Thousands of people have thought of someone, only to hear from them or see them shortly thereafter, without giving any heed to the phenomena involved. These experiences are usually considered coincidences. But isn't the power of thought the real explanation? Anyone with an open mind and willing to read and experiment will sooner or later conclude that the phenomena of psychokinesis and telepathy are realities, and, as investigators have pointed out, that these powers are latent in everyone, though developed to varying degrees.

Hudson, in his *Law of Psychic Phenomena*, originally published in 1893, recounted numerous experiments to prove the existence of telepathy, among them one that made use of playing cards. One member of a group of people was blindfolded, after which another member selected a card, and the others present were told to concentrate on it. The blindfolded person was then asked to name it, according to the first mental impression he received. The results were further proof of the validity of telepathy.

Here is a simple experiment that may be carried out by only three people. Cut from a magazine five colored slips of paper, each about half an inch wide and three inches long. The more vivid the colors (such as bright red or electric blue), the better, but be sure to have them quite distinct from one another. One person should then place them fan-wise between the thumb and forefinger of his right hand, as you would hold a hand of cards. Let a second person touch any one of the colored slips, without being seen by the third person. Immediately after this, the person holding the slips concentrates his mind on the colored slip selected, with a view of communicating the information to the mind of the third person, who is then asked to indicate which slip the second person touched.

The third person's decision must be immediate and spontaneous, and he should either make his mind a blank or be thinking of something entirely remote from the experiment. That is, he should not attempt to guess, deliberate, or *consciously* try to think of the color of the slip selected, but should act immediately upon the first mental impulse he receives. The number of times the third person will name the colored slip selected by the second person will astound you. With a little practice, people who are more or less *en rapport* (such as a husband holding the slips and the wife acting as the third person, after some second person has previously indicated a choice) will make an even higher score of successes. I have seen this done twenty to thirty times without a single miss.

Here again, belief must come into play. The holder of the slips must possess not just the ability to maintain an unwavering concentration, but the strong belief that he can transmit the image of the color to the third person's mind.

Let me interpose a word of caution. This experiment, as well as others outlined in this book, should never be attempted in the presence of scoffers or those who profess disbelief in psychic phenomena. Their negative thoughts may confuse and obstruct the free flow of your own, especially if their skepticism is aggressive. Always remember that belief is a power operating destructively or constructively, depending upon the end to which it is employed. (Dr. Rhine discovered that disbelieving could depress the results in the psychokinesis tests.) In addition, Dr. G. R. Schmeidler of the Harvard Psychological Clinic, where extensive experiments in telepathy have been made, pointed out that subjects who maintain that telepathy is a myth invariably show scores far below chance. Once more, we see the magic of believing in action. Believe that it will work, and it will. Believe that it will not work, and it won't!

The great French astronomer and scientist, Camille Flammarion, was an early exponent of thought-transmission. He held somewhat to the theory later advanced by Professors Eddington and Jeans, claiming that there was mind not only in human and animal life, but in everything—in plants, minerals, even space—and he declared that mind gleams through every atom.

Early in 1947, Dr. Phillips Thomas publicly announced that upon retiring, he intended to devote his time to research in the field of telepathy. Dr. Thomas said, "You may think I'm crazy, but I intend to devote my time to research in this field. We can't conceive scientifically how [telepathy] could come about, but neither can we explain the apparent success of 'mind readers.' "

This announcement caused the Portland *Oregonian* to comment editorially:

> *Before you exclaim, "Ha, another crackpot!" pray reflect that Dr. Phillips Thomas is an eminent scientist who for many years has been research engineer with the Westinghouse Company. Now he elects to become an explorer of that last dark continent, the human mind. . . .*
>
> *It must be evident to the veriest skeptic that Dr. Thomas, international authority on electronics, is convinced—by evidence not lightly to be dismissed—that in our sedulous application to what may be called conventional*

science, we have rather stupidly neglected those challenging phenomena which in times past bore the stigma of sorcery and witchcraft . . .

The proper and rational attitude toward the seeming phenomena of the mind—if that is what they are—is one of scientific inquiry which, though rigorously exacting, will not resist conviction when incontestable proof has been obtained. Actually there can be no such thing as a supernatural phenomenon, but only the manifestation of natural law as yet unknown to us. Nor is it without precedent, this decision of a distinguished scientist to attempt penetration of the unknown continent of the mind . . . Dogmatic disbelief, not infrequently manifested by scientists toward telepathy and similar manifestations, is far from a scientific attitude.

What profit to mankind is there in the quest to which Dr. Thomas presently shall address himself? This is a most difficult question for it may be that the inner secrets are, indeed, inviolable. But if of this research comes a better understanding of ourselves, and of the forces latent in mind, the knowledge might liberate more happiness for the race.

In the late 1940s, much was written about Robert R. Young, the aggressive and energetic chairman of the Board of the Chesapeake & Ohio Railway, and his plans for railroad improvement and development. While I never saw anything in print stating that Mr. Young utilized the subconscious, anyone knowing anything about the subject would conclude that Mr. Young relied greatly upon it for his ideas. An article in *Life* Magazine early in 1947 stated that Mr. Young believed in "extrasensory perception" and that he could "become almost mystical about getting off by himself and 'feeling a truth.' "

Whether it be mind, as we understand the general usage of the word, or electrical vibrations of some kind, the conclusion is that the phenomena themselves embrace and pervade everything, call them what you wish. So when we consider the subconscious of a single individual as only an infinitesimal part of the whole and the vibrations there from extending to and embracing everything, we get a better understanding of psychokinesis, telepathy, and kindred phenomena.

In explaining psychokinesis, Dr. Rhine pointed out that if a person is to be successful in the experiments, there must be a mental attitude of expectancy, concentration of thought, and enthusiasm for the desired results. Again we have the magic of believing at work. The subject must have a prior belief that he can influence the fall of the dice. Belief is the basic factor in the ability to demonstrate psychokinesis (control of mind over matter) and telepathy—as was also confirmed in experiments at Duke University. *New York Herald Tribune* science editor, John J. O'Neill, reported that in these experiments, it was possible to "kid" a person out of his power to demonstrate psychokinesis and telepathy.

He told how a young woman distracted one of the young men attempting to control the fall of the dice, and scoffed at his professed ability to demonstrate his power of mind over matter. She succeeded in injecting such a strong negative factor that she weakened his belief in himself and ruined his score for the day. Mr. O'Neill made an interesting speculation when he went on to say, "The converse of this experiment, still to be made, would test the possibilities for improving the score by a confidence-inspiring pep talk."

In view of the thousands of experiments made at Duke and other universities, it is apparent that scores improve when the experimenters *believe* and are confident of the results. Also, nothing is more logical than that pep talks should help those who lack confidence or belief, and thus should improve their scores. If golf shots can be influenced by mental attitudes or proper visualization, and the "galloping ivories" turn up at the players' mental command, who is to say that events are not influenced by thought? Before us, this field is gradually yielding some secrets of the ancient mysteries. Isn't the so-called luck factor in reality brought about by powerful thought vibrations, rather than coincidence or chance? Writers, long before the experiments at Duke, declared that luck came about from a determined mind—a comination of visualizing, concentrated thought, willing, and believing. Think about this in connection with yourself and the goals you have set for yourself, for in it lies the primary secret of this science.

Gamblers often apply the word "hot" to card players or crap shooters when they have a winning streak. When the hot period wears off, the gamblers either quit the game or begin to lose. What is this streak of good luck? Nothing more than an all-knowing feeling, a deep-rooted belief that they can win. Even in gambling, the magic of believing plays a major role.

Of course, this book is not written for professional gamblers, but for sincere men and women who wish to succeed in life. I refer to games of chance only to provide further evidence that concentrated thought, expectancy, and steadfast belief actually set in motion vibratory forces that bring about material manifestations.

As I stated before, charms, amulets, and talismans have no power in themselves. But those who believe in them firmly and unquestionably tend to develop the kind of force or power now known as psychokinetic. I have tried to make plain how this belief can be developed to take you up the ladder as far as you wish to go. I must point out, though, that it is easy to lose one's belief or faith. Thousands have risen to great heights of success, only to stumble and fall to undreamed-of depths. Others, seeking health, have appeared to be more or less miraculously cured, only to find that their ailments recur years or even months later. There are many weakening factors and influences—all suggestive in nature—which, in unguarded moments, we allow to slip into our subconscious minds. Once there, they begin their destructive work and undo all the good our constructive forces accomplished. So step out in front, head toward the sun. Keep facing it, and dark shadows will not cross your path.

I realize it's difficult for the average person who knows nothing of this subject to accept the idea that all is within. But even as far as the most materialistic person is concerned, nothing exists for him unless he has knowledge of it or unless it becomes fixed in his consciousness. The images created in his mind give reality to the world outside of him. Therefore happiness, sought by many and found by few, is a matter entirely within ourselves. Your environment and the everyday happenings of life have absolutely no effect on your happiness except as you permit mental images of the outside to enter your consciousness. Happiness is wholly independent of position, wealth, or material possessions. It is a state of mind which we ourselves have the power to control—and that control lies with our thinking.

"Consider that everything is opinion, and opinion is in thy power," said the great philosopher Marcus Aurelius Antoninus. "Take away then, when thou choosest, thy opinion; and like a mariner who has doubled the promontory, thou wilt find calm, everything stable, and a waveless bay."

A modern version of this is found in the statement of my seventy-eight-year-old friend, who said, "Distress ensues only when developed by conscious mental attitudes. Disappointments, suppressions, melancholy, depressions, etc.—all are emotional excitations or suggestions from a mode of thinking. If you resisted these emotional tendencies and assert will-power to prevent such influences reaching your consciousness, the foundation of the thought disappears. Consequently, the distress vanishes. Weakness to resist repressing thoughts and imagination arising from emotional reflex both develop from failure of self-control. Stop thinking! Refuse to think that idea or way. Assert *yourself* to be the creator and boss of your own habit of thought—in fact, become unconquerable. No one ever defeated a resolute will. Even death stands still before such a will."

Emerson asked, "What is the hardest task in the world? To think." This is obviously so, when one considers that most of us are victims of mass thinking and feed upon suggestions from others. We all know that the law of cause and effect is inviolable. Yet how many of us ever pause to consider its workings? Many times, the entire course of a man's life has been changed by a single thought coming to him in a flash. History is replete with strong-minded, resolutely willed individuals who, steadfastly holding to their inner convictions, have been able to inspire their fellow-man. In the face of tremendous and determined opposition, they have created literally out of nothing great businesses, huge empires, and altered the whole current of human events.

They had no monopoly of thought-power. You and every other man and woman have it. All you have to do is to use it. You will then become the person you envisage in your imagination; for with the working of the law of cause and effect, you bring into your life the new elements which your most dominant thoughts create from within and attract from outside.

Positive creative thought leads to action and ultimate realization. But the real power, much more than action itself, is the thought. Remember always, "Whatever man can conceive mentally, he can bring into materialization." If the proper mental pictures are created and constantly maintained, health, wealth, and happiness must follow, for the law of cause and effect is immutable.

"Know Thyself." Know your power. *Read* and *reread* this book until it becomes a part of your daily life. Faithfully use the cards and the mirror technique, and you will get results far beyond your fondest expectations. Just believe that there *is* genuine creative magic in believing—and magic there will be, for belief will supply the power for you to succeed in everything you undertake. Back your belief with a resolute will, and you become unconquerable, a master among men—*yourself.*

Index